The Real Story About How the Mounties Always Get their Man
Nobody Said No

Jeff Sallot

James Lorimer & Company, Publishers
Toronto, 1979

ISBN 0-88862-286-4 cloth

Design: Don Fernley

6 5 4 3 2 1   79   80 81 82 83 84 85

Canadian Cataloguing in Publication Data

Sallot, Jeff, 1947-
    Nobody said no

Includes index.
ISBN 0-88862-286-4

1. Canada. Royal Canadian Mounted Police.
2. Police corruption—Canada.   I. Title.

HV8157.S35   363.2'0971   C79-094538-X

James Lorimer & Company, Publishers
Egerton Ryerson Memorial Building
35 Britain Street,
Toronto M5A 1R7, Ontario

Printed and bound in Canada

Contents

For Rosemarie

Acknowledgments

Whether they know it or not, a lot of people helped to make this book a reality. I owe thanks to the colleagues whose work I found to be an invaluable source of information. At the *Globe and Mail*, they include: Lawrence Martin, Richard Cleroux, Marina Strauss, Robert Sheppard, John Marshall, Thomas Claridge and Mary Trueman. Some exceptional reportage on the RCMP was provided by John Sawatsky of the *Vancouver Sun*, Gerard McNeil of Canadian Press and Joe MacAnthony of the CBC's *the fifth estate*. I owe special thanks to reporter Patricia Poirier of La Presse Canadienne, who provided the clearest and most complete coverage in the francophone media. My work was encouraged by an outstanding group of editors at the *Globe and Mail*. They include: Editor-in-chief Richard Doyle, Managing Editor Edward Moser, City Editor Warren Barton and National Editor John King. Jim Lorimer, my publisher, held my hand and helped me through what seemed like endless rewrites. Thanks, too, to Bill Law and Judith Turnbull. My dearest thanks are for Rosemarie Boyle, my best critic, closest colleague and my wife.

All Canadians owe a debt to the members and former members of the RCMP who were courageous enough to let us know about the problem on our hands.

A Note on Sources

The bulk of the research material for this book comes from the public hearings of the Commission of Inquiry Concerning Certain Activities of the Royal Canadian Mounted Police (the McDonald Commission), transcripts of in camera hearings which were later declassified and from declassified documents entered as exhibits in the proceedings. The commission was created by a federal order-in-council on July 6, 1977, and began public hearings in Montreal on December 6, 1977. Hearings were held regularly in Montreal and Ottawa throughout 1978 and 1979 and are continuing at this writing (July 1979). The author attended the public hearings from December 1977 through February 1979. The reader seeking additional information is referred to the public transcripts and exhibits. The commission has made this material available at various locations throughout Canada. A current list of locations can be obtained from: The Commission of Inquiry, P.O. Box 1982, Station B, Ottawa, Ontario, K1P 5R5. Additional research material was obtained from the declassified documents entered as exhibits at the Quebec Commission of Inquiry into the RCMP (the Keable Commission), the final report of the Alberta Commission of Inquiry (the Laycraft Commission), news accounts in the *Globe and Mail*, the *Vancouver Sun* and *Le Devoir*, transcripts of the Canadian Broadcasting Corporation's current affairs program, *the fifth estate*, the final report of the United States

Senate Select Committee regarding intelligence activities (the Church Committee), various reports and documents concerning intelligence and security activities in other Commonwealth countries and interviews with members and former members of the RCMP.

1

Maintiens le Droit

The Royal Canadian Mounted Police is among the most respected institutions in the world. It is the oldest national police force in the Western Hemisphere. Only the Swiss Guard at the Vatican City has a more universally recognized ceremonial uniform. When on parade at Buckingham Palace or at an international exposition in Japan, the scarlet-clad riders of the RCMP never fail to win the enthusiastic cheers of the crowds. Travel guides to Canada feature on their covers lakes, forests, mountains and Mounties. No summertime visit to Ottawa is complete without a snapshot of a Mountie in front of the Peace Tower on Parliament Hill. The scarlet tunic and the broad-brimmed Mountie hat have been symbols of Canada longer than the red Maple Leaf flag. Canadians have more respect for the RCMP than for any other Canadian institution with the exception, perhaps, of the monarchy.

Yet there is a paradox. Canadians can usually recite the names of a half-dozen or more of their sixteen prime ministers, but they would find it difficult to name as many famous Mounties. Most Canadians would know that the late J. Edgar Hoover was the first director of the U.S. Federal Bureau of Investigation. They would fail to react to the names of William L. Higgitt, Maurice Nadon or Robert Simmonds, the last three commissioners of the RCMP.

The RCMP is a cult of impersonality. The force likes it that way. The institution is more important than any of the individuals serving it. Hoover's career demonstrated the dangers of police personality cults. We have learned in Canada only recently that there are dangers just as great in police cults of impersonality.

We know from their testimony at public inquiries that Mounties felt little personal responsibility for their actions. Some of them willingly participated in illegal acts "in the line of duty." They confused duty to the institution with duty to the law. When the conflicts arose their first loyalty was to the force. Law breaking became such an accepted activity that formal policies were established to institutionalize it. There were "protection" policies to reassure men who might be so unfortunate as to get caught.

There are two unofficial mottos of the RCMP. One is: "Don't get caught." Until recently Mounties were rarely caught in their crimes. That motto was pretty well served. The second is: "The Mounties always get their man." That's part of the RCMP mythology, even though the force's unsolved crime rate is about the same as most other police forces. But in pursuit of that noble ideal some Mounties forgot about their third motto, the official one: "Maintiens le Droit"—Uphold the Right.

In spite of all the picture postcards and other RCMP souvenirs, there are relatively few opportunities to see Mounties in their dress uniforms. The scarlet tunic is worn by the Parliament Hill detail only in summer to accommodate the tourists. Most Canadians know Mounties only as the police who patrol the highways in the Atlantic and western provinces. Residents of the two central provinces may go for years without seeing a Mountie. And even in the provinces where the RCMP is the local force, residents see only part of the organization. Part of this is because the RCMP has branches of its organization that the force doesn't want the public to know too much about. There is very deliberate secrecy about the work of one such branch, the Security Service. The reasons are often legitimate. Public exposure of all of its activities would cripple the Security Service. But the secrecy can and has been used to conceal illegal activities. Nor does the general public know a great deal about the work of various sections of the Criminal Investigations Branch. There is less deliberate secrecy in the CIB. Unless someone is the victim or the perpetrator of crimes there are few reasons for a member of the drug squad or the commercial crime section to come calling. However, the secrecy that does exist has contributed to the cover-up of misdeeds.

There is now a great deal more public information about the RCMP because of the Mountie scandals. Much of the initial information was revealed by newspaper and broadcast reporters. And then came a flood of information from four separate official investigations: the federal Commission of Inquiry under Mr. Justice David McDonald; a Quebec Commission of Inquiry under lawyer Jean Keable; an Alberta Royal Commission under Mr. Justice James Laycraft; and an Ontario Royal Commission under Mr. Justice Horace Krever. The McDonald Commission had the broadest mandate and has revealed the most about the structure and activities of the RCMP and, indirectly, about the personalities of the men who failed to "Uphold the Right."

Every single member of the RCMP, from the lowliest recruit to the commissioner at headquarters, fits neatly into an organizational chart. There is an unbroken chain of command and responsibility. The rank structure in ascending order is: recruit, constable, corporal, sergeant, staff sergeant, inspector, superintendent, chief superintendent, assistant commissioner, deputy commissioner, commissioner. There are also titles for certain job functions. A commanding officer of a division, for example, will usually hold the rank of assistant commissioner.

The RCMP is probably one of the most diversified police forces in the world. It is the national police force, the provincial police force in eight of the ten provinces, and the local municipal police force in many of the smaller communities outside Ontario and Quebec. Some of the other provinces used to have their own provincial police but this became a costly proposition and now only Ontario and Quebec maintain their own forces.

The provincial governments are responsible constitutionally for enforcing criminal law. In the four Atlantic and the four western provinces the RCMP is hired on a contract basis by the provincial attorneys-general. In many smaller municipalities in those provinces the local governments also contract with the RCMP for policing. In the larger cities which have their own city police the policemen are responsible to a chief and through the chief to a board or police commission and then ultimately to the municipal council. The provincial police of Quebec and Ontario are responsible to provincial police commissions and the attorneys-general. In the Atlantic and western provinces, however, there are in effect two chains of command. In theory, the RCMP under contract are always responsible to the provincial attorneys-general. But because of the RCMP Act, a federal statute, and the RCMP chain of command, the contract Mounties are also responsible to headquarters in Ottawa and to their commissioner. Usually there is no difficulty in this arrangement. But when a conflict arises the natural inclination of the Mountie is to put his loyalty to the force and headquarters above his responsibilities to the provincial authorities. Most Mounties are career men and they know that they may be transferred to several provinces during their years with the force. A strong sense of responsibility or duty to any one provincial government or attorney-general often doesn't develop. In addition, since provincial governments can change at election time, the political masters are sometimes seen as transients. The only thing unchanging in a Mountie's life is the force.

This unwavering loyalty to the force has caused some problems for at least one provincial attorney-general. James Foster, the former attorney-general of Alberta, fell out with the force during a complex white-collar crime investigation. Foster felt that some of the evidence had been obtained improperly and that the prosecution should be dropped. The RCMP never told Foster that evidence was obtained as the result of a secret agreement between the force and the Department of National Revenue. Foster felt he had been deceived and he established a provincial inquiry—the Laycraft Commission—to try to sort out the mess. Relations between Foster and the Mounties deteriorated to the point where Foster felt the RCMP was spying on him and secretly bugging his conversations, a charge denied by the force. The case illustrated that when the RCMP is trying to serve two masters the provincial authorities are likely to get the short end of the stick.

There is another danger in the dual loyalty arrangement. If the RCMP as provincial police discover that one of their members is acting illegally they are faced with having to decide whether or not to report it to the provincial attorney-general responsible for criminal prosecutions in the province. RCMP headquarters has had an established policy of trying to protect members caught in illegal acts "in the line of duty." Part of that policy was to try to persuade a provincial attorney-general not to press charges, and that presumes that the attorney-general first knows about the illegal activity. Although it doesn't appear in written policy documents, it doesn't take a clever mind to figure out that it is easier simply not to tell an attorney-general who doesn't have his own provincial police at his disposal.

Within the RCMP there are two separate command structures leading to the office of the commissioner: the Security Service, known prior to 1970 as the Security and Intelligence Branch (SIB), and the Criminal Investigations Branch (CIB).

The CIB is subdivided into two. There is Criminal Investigations—General. Its members are the Mounties most Canadians are familiar with. They include the contract police in the Atlantic and western provinces and smaller municipalities. They enforce traffic laws, investigate minor crimes, handle domestic disputes and perform all of the routine duties of local police. They have been untainted by the recent scandals. The general section also maintains liaison with Interpol, the international clearing house for police information in Paris. It also includes the legal branch, the RCMP's group of five or six in-house lawyers, and a section employed in the tracking down of illegal immigrants.

The second CIB subdivision is Criminal Investigations—Federal. This includes customs and excise investigators, the various drug squads, the national crime intelligence branch, which is heavily involved in organized crime investigations, and the commercial crime branch whose duties include investigating frauds and counterfeiting cases.

Most Mounties spend their entire careers in the CIB. The usual progression is from basic training in Regina to a posting at a contract policing detachment, and then perhaps promotion and assignment to a position of authority in a larger detachment. If the Mountie shows some special talent or inclination for undercover work he may be assigned to a drug squad. If he shows ability as a good general investigator of routine crimes he may advance to one of the specialized units within the commercial crime branch or the national crime intelligence branch. If he's a good administrator he may advance through the ranks to become an officer in charge of his own detachment and eventually a commanding officer of a division, a geographical region usually comprising an entire province. (Ontario is divided into two divisions. Alberta, the Yukon and the Northwest Territories comprise one division.)

All career advancement is through the ranks. You can't join as an officer no matter what your qualifications. The educational background of recruits ranges from the minimum Grade 12 requirement to university degrees. Most, however, do not have university training. All recruits start with the basic training of about six months at the Regina training depot. In Ottawa, the headquarters staff is just part of a large federal bureaucracy in that city. Regina is the hometown of the RCMP and many people there feel that the RCMP has put their town on the map. Even the McDonald's hamburger restaurant in Regina commemorates the RCMP with giant wall posters of Hollywood movies featuring the Mounties.

The RCMP was created in 1873 as a semi-military organization. The rigid military discipline of the force remains a part of the tradition that is first learned by recruits at Regina. Seasoned Mounties call it "teaching them to wear the saddle." Unlike many military organizations, the RCMP doesn't have a university or college academy to train an officer corps. In recent years, however, the force has placed a greater emphasis on advanced education and sends some of its men back for university studies after they have served in the ranks. The typical recruit is likely to be a fresh high-school graduate from a smaller urban centre or a rural area. His only previous exposure to policemen may be what he has seen of the RCMP as he grew up. For years the RCMP cut itself off from a potential source of more mature recruits because it wouldn't hire already married men. There has been more recruiting of people from varied backgrounds and experiences in recent years. But the officer ranks are still dominated by men who were cut from the same cloth. Former Solicitor-General Jean-Pierre Goyer told the McDonald Commission that some Mounties bragged that "the RCMP is a WASP organization" and were proud of it.

The Security Service gets its men from the ranks of the CIB. There are varying opinions within the force about the status of Security Service men. Many older CIB officers look at the Security Service with disdain. They see it as the place where those who couldn't cut it were relegated to the drudgery of routine background investigations of civil service applicants who need security clearance. "National security" work once meant little more than screening immigration applicants from Eastern Europe.

Events of the last decade have altered the way the Security Service is perceived, particularly by younger Mounties. The Security Service was thrown into the big league when the October Crisis of 1970 cast the international spotlight on Canada. The security planning for the 1976 Montreal Olympic Games got a lot of attention because of the terrorist murders of Israeli athletes at the 1972 Munich Olympics. The fact that the Montreal games passed without incident was boasted of by the RCMP. The Mounties are also particularly proud of the tight security protection afforded former U.S. President Richard Nixon during his visit to Ottawa in 1971. Arthur Bremer, the man who later shot and wounded Alabama Governor George Wallace, was in the crowd on Parliament Hill, stalking Nixon with a gun. Mountie security was so good that Bremer never got a chance to fire. The RCMP made a training film of the security efforts that went into the Nixon visit. Some Mounties think the film is so interesting that it should be declassified and shown to the general public.

The Security Service is very secretive about its organizational structure. The designations for various branches are changed periodically so that if classified documents leak it will be difficult for outsiders to figure out what operational branch has been involved in a certain type of activity. For example, "F Ops" (F-section Operations) may be the designation for the security records branch one year and for the communications intelligence branch two years later. The number of men assigned to the various branches is also classified information. The theory is that if hostile intelligence services know the manpower strengths of branches they can figure out where the Security Service is concentrating its interest and where the weaknesses are. At the top of the organization is the director-general. In theory he reports to the commissioner. But in practice he and the commissioner are equals and both report to the solicitor-general. In cases of emergency or where highly sensitive matters are involved the director-general has direct access to the prime minister.

Historically the director-general has been a career officer like William L. Higgitt who went on to become commissioner in 1969. But the two most recent appointments have been from outside the force. This was a concession to the recommendations for a civilian security agency made by a Royal Commission in 1969. The RCMP wanted to retain the Security Service within the force. The government agreed, but appointed John Starnes, a civilian, as director-general. He was succeeded in 1973 by General Michael Dare, a military man.

Beneath the director-general are three deputies. The deputies usually hold the rank of assistant commissioner — a rank just two levels below the commissioner. In 1976 the deputy director-general for Operational Services was responsible for "E Ops" (communications intelligence), "F Ops" (security records), "I Ops" (surveillance), "J Ops" (technical development and computer data processing). The deputy director-general for administration and personnel is responsible for bureaucratic functions, such as financial and supply services, staff training and development and hirings. He does have one other significant responsibility — internal security. This usually involves routine physical protection of classified material, installation of office safes and locks on doors. In the rare cases when documents are leaked the internal security branch assumes a greater importance, having the duty to determine how the leak occurred. The Security Service uses an ingenious method of tracking down the source of leaked cypher communications between headquarters and field units. Many cypher Telex messages are sent to all field units across Canada but each unit will receive a slightly different copy of the message. The differences are generally deliberate typographical errors. Montreal, for example, may get a message with the word "the" in the second paragraph spelled "teh," while Vancouver may get the same message with the word "and" in the final paragraph spelled "adn." By checking the leaked document it's easy to isolate a smaller group of suspects.

The deputy director-general for operations has the most important responsibilities. His men are the people who actually carry
out investigations and maintain liaison with foreign intelligence
services, such as the U.S. Central Intelligence Agency. In 1976 the
"DDG-Ops" had under his command six separate sections. "A
Ops" had the tiresome job of security screening for federal civil
servants. "B Ops" was the counterintelligence unit which tried to
ferret out foreign spies and kept track of the intelligence officers
operating under the diplomatic cover of Eastern Block embassies
in Ottawa. "D Ops" was security intelligence, the unit responsible
for investigating suspected terrorist and subversive groups and
individuals. "H Ops" was Far East counterintelligence, a unit set
up specifically to watch the Chinese Embassy and its staff. "L
Ops" was human source development, the recruitment of informers. In 1970 a special unit called "G Ops" was created. It had
as its specific responsibility Quebec terrorist groups such as the
Front de Libération du Québec (FLQ), and separatist movements, such as the Parti Québécois. "G Ops" was absorbed back
into "D Ops" in 1974.

Each of the operation branches at headquarters had its corre-
sponding sections in the field. "G Ops," also known as G-branch at
headquarters, had a G-section in Montreal and Quebec City. Montreal's G-section became known as the dirty tricks squad because of
its illegal activities—break-ins, arson, theft of dynamite and so on.
Each section was responsible to a Security Service officer, usually
with the rank of superintendent or chief superintendent. On paper
the Security Service field sections were responsible to the commanding officer for their geographical division. In practice, they
reported directly to Security Service headquarters in Ottawa.

G-section in Montreal was subdivided four ways. G-1 was the
section's officer-in-charge, Insp. Donald Cobb, and his staff. G-2
was responsible for surveillance of FLQ suspects. It was headed
by Staff Sgt. Donald McCleery. G-3 was a paperwork group
which maintained files on separatists and trade unionists in
Quebec. G-4 was responsible for recruiting informers and attempting to infiltrate separatist groups.

Supervising the force was supposed to be the responsibility of
the solicitor-general. The portfolio was created in the mid-1960s

to relieve some of the burdens of the justice minister, who until then had been the minister in charge of the force. The solicitor-general's job was generally considered a junior portfolio. The position was occupied at various times by people on their way up, such as John Turner and Francis Fox, or some of the lesser lights from the Liberal back benches who could no longer be kept out of the cabinet. In the ten years between 1968 and 1978 there were no fewer than six different solicitors-general. Those holding this office also had the responsibilities of federal prisons and they seemed to have little time or inclination to keep close tabs on the RCMP.

The solicitor-general is responsible to Parliament. Parliamentary scrutiny was limited to the question period and occasional hearings at the Commons Justice and Legal Affairs Committee. The committee, as with all parliamentary committees, was overworked and had little time to devote to the RCMP. Committee members were also hamstrung by rules that limited the time for questioning witnesses and by the lack of independent support staff, counsel and investigators. In 1973, when the committee was debating a police wiretap bill and might have given some close scrutiny to the activities of the RCMP, committee members were also burdened with a heavy workload that included prison reform and capital punishment issues. There was no elected representative or other civilian whose exclusive duty it was to act as a watchdog of the RCMP. The RCMP had the trust and confidence of ministers and other parliamentarians and as a result had a free hand to get into trouble.

In 1969 William Leonard "Len" Higgitt made it to the top as the fourteenth commissioner of the RCMP. He served as commissioner until the end of the RCMP's centennial year, 1973. This was also the period of the greatest illegal activity undertaken by the Mounties. Higgitt knew about some of it at the time. He was the kind of officer who wore the uniform well. A trim man, even in his fifties, he looked every inch the policeman who had risen to the top because of intelligence, dedication and honest hard work. His sharp facial features betrayed no hint that he knew about skeletons in the closet. But in thirty-six years with the force he had learned a lot, especially about how to keep secrets.

Higgitt was typical of his generation of officers. He was a small-town boy from Anerley, Saskatchewan. He joined the force two years before World War II at the age of twenty. After basic training at Regina he spent his first two years of duty in his native province. Early in the war he was posted to Ottawa where he was initiated into the secret world of security and intelligence work. He was one of the men who worked on the Gouzenko case after the war. He was commissioned as an officer in 1952 and performed general police administrative duties for the next five years in Toronto and Montreal. But by 1957 he was back in the Security and Intelligence Branch where he remained until his appointment as commissioner twelve years later. His specialty was counterintelligence and his duties were almost exclusively at Ottawa headquarters. Higgitt, however, did get one of the prestigious foreign assignments, three years in London as the liaison officer with British intelligence.

Higgitt could be blunt when he wanted to be. He angered Prime Minister Trudeau in 1969 by telling a news conference that closer links with mainland China and the opening of a Chinese embassy in Ottawa would increase national security problems for the RCMP. Trudeau later told reporters that the new commissioner was "allowed one mistake." But Higgitt could also be evasive. He deftly dodged questions before the Justice and Legal Affairs Committee when members of Parliament wanted to know if the RCMP conducted wiretaps. And he was tough to pin down at the McDonald Commission when he was asked for specifics on where and when cabinet ministers might have been told of illegal activities as he claimed. Len Higgitt had a way with words.

Higgitt didn't like it very much when the Trudeau government decided in 1970 that it was going to appoint an outsider as the director-general of the Security Service. But he held his tongue and if it had to be an outsider, Higgitt told the McDonald Commission, there could have been no better choice than John Starnes.

Starnes' appointment was made a bit more palatable for the force by the fact that he had a background in military intelligence and he was distantly related to Cortlandt Starnes, the RCMP commissioner from 1923 to 1931. But Starnes was more in keeping with Trudeau's image of the chief of intelligence, an image which was in the elitist tradition of British intelligence and the U.S. Central Intelligence Agency, favoring the recruitment of the sons of the upper class from the very best universities. Starnes was a scion of the Canadian establishment. His grandfather had been a Liberal member of Parliament. Starnes was educated at one of the best universities in Europe. During the war he went overseas with the Blackwatch Regiment. In London his talents were spotted and he was seconded to the Canadian Intelligence Corps and was put in charge of administration.

Starnes has said his forte is administration. In technical matters "I wouldn't know one end of a microscope from another" and he could never remember what all the various code words meant. Tall and aristocratic, Starnes looks like a diplomat, which is exactly what he became after the war. He joined the External Affairs Department and in 1948 he was part of the Canadian mission to the United Nations. He served twice in Germany, the second posting as the Canadian ambassador, and went on to Cairo as ambassador to Egypt in 1966. In 1967 he was back home in Ottawa as the assistant undersecretary of state for External Affairs — the second highest civil service rank in that department. This job involved a tight liaison with the RCMP on foreign intelligence matters.

Starnes learned of RCMP illegal activities shortly after he became director-general of the Security Service. He knew of break-ins, but there were other activities, such as illegal mail openings, that the Mounties never told him about. Starnes says covert operations weren't really his specialty. He was an administrator.

Starnes' man in Montreal was Insp. Donald Cobb, the officer in charge of G-section, the anti-separatist unit. The men seemed to get along well together. Cobb had come up through the ranks, but he had an air of refined sophistication about him. He read psychological and political essays to try to understand the roots of urban terrorism. He was from Montreal but didn't really learn French until he was posted to Europe as an RCMP liaison officer. He became fluently bilingual. He joined the force with just a high-school education but the Mounties later sent him back to university to study social sciences. He joined the Security Service after being in the force just five years. There was a quick string of important foreign jobs in France, Italy and Germany. He first saw urban terrorists at work when a neighbour of his in France was gunned down by Algerians.

Cobb has subtle good looks and, like Higgitt, wears the uniform well. The force had great plans for him. At one time there was talk at headquarters that Cobb would someday make commissioner. He seemed to be the perfect blend between a man with Starnes' intellectual capacity and Higgitt's life-long dedication to the force.

Cobb's man in charge of G-2 was Staff Sgt. Donald McCleery, a tough breed of cop who didn't have much use for things like organizational charts and written job descriptions. McCleery knew how to talk tough and get the job done. While Cobb was away studying at Laval University, McCleery and his men were in the heat of the action during the October Crisis. He is generally credited with being one of the key figures in tracking down the FLQ terrorists of the October Crisis. He drove his men hard and himself even harder.

And one of McCleery's men was Const. Robert Samson, a bit of an enigma. Like McCleery, Samson liked the action. But he seemed to make other people nervous, particularly the policemen from other forces with whom he worked on anti-terrorist operations. From the Security Service's point of view, Samson had one fatal flaw. He talked about an RCMP break-in.

Higgitt, Starnes, Cobb, McCleery and Samson—from the commissioner to the constable—were men who acted out of a sense of duty. The officers—Higgitt, Starnes and Cobb—knew about unlawful activities and approved. The noncommissioned officer—McCleery—issued a direct order leading to an illegal act. And at the bottom were men like Samson, the foot soldiers who carried out orders without question. This was the command structure of Canada's Royal Canadian Mounted Police.

2

Nobody Said No

The summer of 1972 passed quietly for most people in Quebec. The October Crisis of 1970 was a fading memory and there were few outward signs of social unrest in the province. But below the surface there were hidden events. Members of the combined anti-terrorist unit of the Royal Canadian Mounted Police Security Service, the Montreal police and the Quebec Police Force were keeping a close watch on the activities of a small group of dedicated radicals who continued the separatist struggle from offices in a drab, grey stone three-storey building at 3459 St. Hubert Street in working-class east-end Montreal. The police believed that if the Front de Libération du Québec was to experience a renaissance and again plunge Quebec society into chaos and crisis, the first stirrings would be seen here at offices leased by L'Agence-Presse Libre du Québec, the APLQ.

The APLQ waged its revolution with words. Its publication, the *Bulletin,* was filled with Marxist rhetoric and stories about the "class struggle" between the capitalists and Quebec's working class. Members of this journalistic collective barely kept body and soul together with the small amounts they received from subscriptions and, ironically, federal funds from the Opportunities for Youth and Local Initiatives Program. The APLQ was never a serious threat to "national security," that is, the status quo.

The police were much more worried about an allied group, the Movement for the Defence of Political Prisoners of Quebec. Many of the same people who were active with the APLQ were also members of the MDPPQ. The MDPPQ was basically a fund-raising organization to help pay the legal bills for jailed FLQ members. Separatists and sympathizers who shared the Marxist ideology of the FLQ contributed whatever sums they could during 1971 and early 1972. But by the summer and early fall of 1972 most of the separatist action had been channelled into mainstream politics and the rising star of René Lévesque and his Parti Québécois. The MDPPQ was on its last legs and probably would have disappeared before the end of the year. The police decided to hasten the process.

The APLQ shared its leased office space with the MDPPQ. The building on St. Hubert Street was well known to the police. Montreal police had been inside it at least twice to plant bugs. The RCMP Security Service had its own "cobra source," that is, a wiretap on the APLQ phone. The activities of the groups were also known to at least one very senior politician in Ottawa. Jean-Pierre Goyer, as solicitor-general, was at the time the federal minister reponsible for the RCMP and its Security Service. He saw the intelligence reports and each month he reviewed the list of the RCMP's currently operational wiretaps and bugs. The APLQ had been on the list for many months.

The bugs and the phone tap were of limited intelligence value. Paranoia was rampant in the semi-underground separatist movement and people were cautious about what they said on the phone or in a building that might be bugged. Security Service attempts to recruit paid informers were not all that successful. Infiltration by the Security Service was impossible. But the Security Service picked up one piece of intriguing information. Louise Vandelac, a member of the APLQ, was waiting for a letter from Cuba.

The Security Service intercepted a CNCP Telecommunications message to Vandelac from Jacques Cossette-Trudel, one of the FLQ kidnappers of British Trade Commissioner James Cross. From his exile in Cuba, Cossette-Trudel told Vandelac that she should expect a courier to arrive in Montreal with an important letter for her and the others in the movement. This letter became an obsession for one of the members of the combined anti-terrorist unit. Security Service Const. Robert Samson desperately wanted to get his hands on it.

Samson had been a Mountie for less than five years. The young man, in his late twenties, didn't seem to fit the part of an intelligence operative. He was tall, slim and sandy haired. His manner seemed almost meek. But he managed to make good contacts in the underworld and he was eager to please his superiors. He was a central figure in the planning of combined anti-terrorist unit operations during the fall of 1972.

The combined anti-terrorist unit was an odd group of policemen. The members of the three forces came from different backgrounds and different police traditions. The Montreal police were tough, street-wise cops who made their careers by cultivating contacts among the pimps, hookers and petty crooks in the big city. Successful undercover vice-squad or plainclothes work led to promotion to the intelligence unit. The Quebec Police Force was basically a rural force. Rookies got their start as highway patrolmen and traffic cops. But the QPF also placed greater emphasis than did the Montreal police on its intelligence work. Its files were more sophisticated and its men had greater access to electronic surveillance equipment. The RCMP was the senior force. Its Security Service had important contacts with foreign intelligence services. The Mounties were subject to much more rigid paramilitary command structures and discipline. The compensation was the glamour associated with "national security" work. The Mounties also had more money to spend on informers and sophisticated equipment. And it seemed to the members of the other two forces that the Mounties had much greater freedom to roam where they wanted, to search what they wanted and to do almost anything they wanted to do in the name of national security. But like the members of the QPF, the RCMP Security Service men generally cut their teeth in small, semi-rural detachments outside Quebec and Ontario.

There was minimal cooperation between the three forces prior to the October Crisis of 1970. But the investigations into the Cross kidnapping and the murder of Quebec Labour Minister Pierre

Laporte threw the men of the three forces into close contact. There was still some distance between the three senior commands, but the men in the field got to know each other, worked well together and enjoyed each other's company. The combined anti-terrorist unit began as a clearing-house operation for intelligence reports about the FLQ. Largely as the result of the desires of the lower-ranking field-unit members, it grew to the point where joint operations and raids were planned and carried out.

There was a weakness in this setup, however. There was no overall command. In theory each man was still responsible to his superiors in his own force. But in practice no senior officer from any force was in charge or exercised direct supervisory control over all the men. Furthermore, on a day-to-day basis the men, none of whom ranked higher than sergeant, were beyond the control and discipline of their own superiors. Fanciful ideas took on lives of their own to become full-fledged operational plans. There was nobody to take a sober second look at the plans to see if they were legal or not. There was nobody to say no.

The men of the combined unit hung out at Montreal police headquarters. It was there in September 1972 that the plan for a break-in at the APLQ offices was mapped out. The men gave the plan a romantic code name, Operation Bricole. In rough translation, Bricole means Odd Job, the name of a villain in a James Bond movie.

The actual objectives of Operation Bricole are still obscure. The Montreal police and the QPF members thought that they were playing a support role to help the Security Service obtain the Cossette-Trudel letter to Vandelac. They thought this was a national security case and that the Mounties were taking the lead role. The Mounties thought the forces were all in it together equally and that their prime objective was to disrupt and, hopefully, deal a death blow to the MDPPQ. The Security Service knew that the MDPPQ was in a sorry state and all it would take was a little push to finish it off. The Mounties hoped to accomplish this by breaking into the St. Hubert Street building and stealing the MDPPQ's documents, especially its lists of members and contributors. The Cossette-Trudel letter was a secondary objective for all of the Mounties, except for Samson. It never seemed to occur to the men that they might be able to get what they wanted with a legal search warrant authorized by a judge.

The Operation Bricole planning was haphazard. It violated one of the cardinal rules of clandestine dirty tricks operations—too many people were involved. There was too great a chance that someone would eventually talk. The operation also lacked any clear backup plan to shift the blame for the break-in and theft from the police, who would be the obvious suspects, to someone else. The men thought they could pull this off by planting some of the stolen documents with a member of the Milice Republicaine, a rival separatist group with right-wing tendencies. The Milice Republicaine had asked the APLQ and the MDPPQ for lists of supporters but had been turned down. But the men didn't devise a method to plant the documents or to let their whereabouts be known to the APLQ and the MDPPQ.

At another routine get-together of the combined unit on September 29, Samson arrived with an exciting piece of news. The Mounties' cobra wiretap was paying dividends. From it the Security Service had learned the combination to the safe at the APLQ offices. Samson took Montreal police Sgt. Claude Marcotte aside. Samson wanted the Montreal police to take this information and conduct the raid on their own. Marcotte objected. If there was to be a raid they would all be in on it together. The two men returned to the meeting and the planning continued.

Samson spent a lot of his time at Montreal police headquarters unaccompanied by any other member of the Security Service. As the planning reached its final stages he orally briefed four of his superiors at the RCMP offices. He met with Insp. Claude Vermette, Staff Sgt. François d'Entremont, Sgt. Henri Pelletier and Sgt. Hugues Fortin. Vermette, the senior officer, had just recently been appointed to his new job. He hadn't fully familiarized himself with the operational files and he only vaguely knew what the APLQ and the MDPPQ were all about. He had no objections to the break-in plans in principle. Everybody knew that it was to be an operation without any legal authorization, such as a search warrant, and "nobody said no," Pelletier told the McDonald Commission. Vermette was willing to go along with it if it was okay with the other two forces. But he wanted something more formal before him, something in writing. He sent Samson and the others away with instructions to come back with a written operational report and to include other possible options to a break-in. He assigned Sgt. Claude Brodeur to help Samson.

Vermette, a tall, square-jawed career Mountie, was planning a Thanksgiving weekend hunting trip with his close personal friend and boss, Chief Supt. J.L. Forest, the officer in charge of Security Service operations in Quebec. Vermette thought that it would take Samson and Brodeur a couple of weeks to come back with a report. But within the next few days Vermette mentioned the plan in conversation with his hunting partner. Vermette said that Operation Bricole would involve a clandestine break-in, without a search warrant, and the seizure of documents. Forest didn't seem to be surprised. He just listened and said to continue the study.

At about this time there was a phone conversation between Vermette and his counterpart at the QPF, Insp. Jean Coutellier. Operation Bricole was discussed. Vermette can't remember the details, but Coutellier says that he got the distinct impression that Vermette was sanctioning the break-in. That was good enough for Coutellier. He authorized QPF participation because he had faith in the judgment of the Security Service and he felt that the participation of the RCMP was a guarantee that the operation was necessary for national security reasons despite the apparent illegality.

Detective Lt. Roger Cormier, the head of the Montreal police intelligence department, had no difficulty making up his mind. His men were in. He thought the operation must be legal because he believed, wrongly, that the Mounties had special search and seizure powers in national security cases and didn't need a search warrant.

During the early afternoon of Wednesday, October 4, Vermette and Forest left the RCMP offices and packed up their gear for their extended hunting trip in eastern Quebec. They were out of contact with their office until the following Tuesday. At just about that same time Samson was again at Montreal police headquarters, helping to put the final touches on the break-in plans. A timetable was set. The break-in was to occur in less than sixty hours. Tasks were assigned and a final meeting was set for Friday.

Sergeant Brodeur went with Samson to the final meeting. It was the first planning meeting he had attended and Brodeur was surprised at how far along the plot had progressed. He was nervous. When Brodeur learned that the raid was scheduled for that night he excused himself and went to look for a phone. From an adjacent office he called Sergeant Pelletier at the RCMP. Both Brodeur and Pelletier knew that the search was to be without a warrant. That had been understood clearly when Samson briefed Vermette. There had been no objection voiced by Vermette. But Vermette was away and he hadn't seen a final written report. Pelletier was worried. The two sergeants talked for about fifteen minutes while the men from the other two forces waited in the next office, puzzled by why the Mounties were apparently delaying.

Samson excused himself and went next door to talk with Brodeur. Samson was insistent. If the Security Service backed out at this late hour the other two forces would conduct the raid anyway and the RCMP would lose face. What's more, the close cooperative relationship that had grown up during the past two years would be badly damaged. Brodeur passed this view along to Pelletier. Pelletier didn't want to take responsibility. But he told Brodeur to go back to the meeting and if Pelletier didn't phone back within five minutes Brodeur and Samson were to assume that they had the go-ahead. Pelletier rang off and hurried down the hall to find Insp. Donald Cobb.

Cobb had no way of knowing it at the time, but he was about to be asked to make the most important decision in his twenty-two-year career with the RCMP. It may have been one of the most important decisions ever made by a single officer of the RCMP. It had far-reaching repercussions for the entire force, the federal government and certainly his own career. Cobb later told the McDonald Commission that he decided to authorize the break-in "even if some aspects left me with an uncomfortable feeling."

Cobb was a different kind of cop. He was reflective, at times almost philosophical, about his work. Tall, attractive and possessed of a Gary Cooper type of charm, Cobb looked and talked like central casting's version of a private eye. Most officers of his age and rank had toiled for years in rural detachments before attaining the more prestigious postings in the big cities. The others had earned their spurs on lonely traffic patrols of long stretches of the Trans-Canada Highway or breaking up Saturday night fights in the hamlets of New Brunswick or Manitoba. Many had come from small towns, towns where the members of the local RCMP detachment were as well known and respected as the minister or the school teacher.

Cobb was a city boy. He grew up in Montreal's Irish-Catholic neighbourhood of Notre-Dame-de-Grace. After high school he worked for awhile as an office clerk in the publicity department at Canadian Pacific Airlines Limited. But he wanted something more. He joined the force and was shipped off to the training depot in Regina. Upon graduation, Cobb was transferred back to Montreal. He was selected for security work early in his career and assigned to the special branch, the forerunner of the Security Service, in 1954 after only four years' experience as a policeman.

Then came a string of prestigious foreign assignments — France, Italy and Germany where he worked in the visa control department and as a liaison officer with European intelligence services. His first assignment to Ottawa headquarters was in 1962 when he worked as an analyst in D-section, the countersubversion unit. During the late 1960s he was again in Montreal, this time as the inspector in charge of local security operations. He witnessed the full flowering of Quebec's Quiet Revolution and he saw the emergence of a dangerous new element in Quebec politics, the FLQ terrorists' bombings. But it was his fate to miss the big operation, the October Crisis of 1970. Cobb had been sent by the force to study social sciences that fall at Laval University. He was intelligent, articulate in English and French, and part of a new breed of Mountie who could discuss the technical complexities of a wiretap as easily as the Marxist theory of history. He continued to rise through the ranks.

The October Crisis revealed weaknesses in Security Service operations. When he returned from his studies, Cobb was assigned to the restructuring of G-Section, the new Quebec anti-terrorist unit that had grown out of D-section during the October Crisis. His performance again pleased his superiors in Ottawa. By September 1972 they had marked him for another important assignment. In a few weeks he was to move to Ottawa as an aide to Deputy Solicitor-General Roger Tasse. In this position he would be near political power as the force's closest representative in the ministry. There was already speculation at headquarters that Cobb would be the next commissioner.

The transition of the G-section command from Cobb to Vermette was complete in Montreal. Cobb was biding his time until after the November federal election when he would move to Ottawa. He kept himself busy with administrative tasks.

Sergeant Pelletier appeared agitated as he entered Cobb's office that Friday afternoon at about 4:15 p.m. While Vermette was away Cobb was the senior in charge and the one to handle problems. Pelletier wasn't able to get to the point. He didn't know how much Cobb already knew about Operation Bricole. He didn't know how much he should say. The Security Service operated on a strict "need-to-know" basis and nobody discussed their work with others unless they had to get an approval to get the job done. This reduced the risk of leaks. Pelletier was in a tight spot. He knew he didn't have the authority to okay the break-in. He finally gave Cobb a quick rundown and went home for the weekend.

It was Cobb's turn to worry. From his previous experience he was well aware of the people involved in the APLQ and the MDPPQ. He considered them dangerous. There were certainly benefits to be gained from Operation Bricole—intelligence and potential disruption of the groups. But those same benefits were available to the police through a legal search warrant. Time was running short. Cobb thought that a delay might damage the entire operation. There was also the worry of losing face with the other forces and souring the cooperative relationships that had been so slow to cultivate.

Cobb set aside the ethical and legal questions and for a moment considered Operation Bricole from a strictly tactical point of view. It seemed that every contingency had been considered right down to the lock picking. But he was uncomfortable with the fact that so many people were involved, probably a dozen. And many more might know about it. "They provided for every contingency except the possibility that one man might talk, like Samson did," Cobb later told the McDonald Commission.

Cobb decided to inform John Starnes, his friend and the director-general of the Security Service. Cobb didn't think he needed any approval from Starnes, he just wanted the director-general to be told what was about to happen. Cobb got Starnes' secretary, who told him that the director-general was away in Halifax and wouldn't be back in Ottawa until Tuesday morning. Cobb said thank you and hung up. He didn't try to phone any of Starnes' deputies. At 4:45 p.m. Cobb left his office and informed the skeleton crew of operational staff members that he was going home and would be there all weekend if he was needed. The last chance for somebody to say no had passed.

It was quiet on St. Hubert Street as the operational team set out after midnight. There were few apartments or homes in the area. Each man was dressed in plain clothes and some wore rubber-soled shoes to deaden their footsteps. Those who were to go inside brought along gloves so that they wouldn't leave fingerprints. They had hockey equipment bags to stuff documents into. Two Montreal police officers rode in a truck that was rented with false identity papers so that it couldn't be traced. One officer drove while another monitored the police band of a portable radio to make sure no errant squad cars wandered into the area. Sergeant Brodeur acted as a lookout circling the block slowly in an unmarked, radio-equipped car. A member of the QPF and a Montreal policeman waited outside to load the hockey bags into the truck while a member of the Security Service monitored the cobra source at the RCMP offices to make sure nobody was inside the target building. A Montreal police locksmith opened the place up. Three men went inside—Samson and two members of the QPF and Montreal police. The trio worked quickly and quietly, going through filing cabinets and desk drawers. In the semidarkness, working only with the illumination of flashlights, the searchers couldn't examine all that they were packing into the hockey bags. They grabbed every piece of paper they could see. They took thousands of documents, many of them back issues of the APLQ *Bulletin* and other radical publications with little or no intelligence value. The last hockey bag was zipped up and tossed into the truck. The men left as quietly as they had arrived. There wasn't a hitch. The job took twenty minutes.

The team headed back to Montreal police headquarters to store the goods. Detective Lieutenant Cormier was surprised by all that the men had taken. There was too much. It couldn't be kept safely at Montreal police intelligence unit offices because it would clutter things up. Brodeur tried to get the okay to take the documents to RCMP offices. But for some reason that he didn't understand the permission was denied. Brodeur volunteered to keep the documents in his basement where his wife and their Doberman pinscher could safeguard things. "I have a very aggressive wife and she has an aggressive Doberman," Brodeur told the McDonald Commission. This seemed to solve the problem.

The men had anticipated that nobody would show up at the APLQ offices until Tuesday morning so that the trail would be cold by the time the break-in was discovered. But a member of the group did turn up on Saturday. The incident was reported to Station 16, the nearest Montreal police station, and a routine breaking and entering investigation was started. Members of the APLQ and the MDPPQ also did something else. They sent telegrams to senior politicians and police officials informing them that police dirty work was suspected. Further, they called a press conference and alleged that they had been the victim of a police break-in. News editors didn't take the allegations seriously. The radicals didn't have any proof that it was the police and not somebody else who had staged the break-in. The stories were buried on back pages. Federal election news took priority on page one.

Vermette's hunting trip with Forest was a success. An experienced deer hunter, Vermette bagged his first moose that weekend, a 1,100-pound beauty. He was feeling pretty good about it and was anxious to tell the others at the office how he felled the animal with the second shot from his war surplus .303 Lee-Enfield rifle. His mood changed when he arrived Tuesday morning and learned that Operation Bricole had been carried out. Cobb gave him the details. Vermette was surprised that events had transpired that quickly.

The cover-up began that morning in Montreal, Quebec City and Ottawa. Senior officials of the Montreal police had received one of the accusatory telegrams from the APLQ and the MDPPQ. They didn't respond. They handled the affair like any other break-in. A detective from Station 16 called Detective Lieutenant Cormier at the intelligence unit to ask if Cormier or any of his men knew anything about the incident on St. Hubert Street. Cormier didn't think it was any of the detective's business and he didn't tell him a thing. That effectively ended the official Montreal police investigation.

Quebec Justice Minister Jérôme Choquette, responsible for the QPF, got one of the telegrams. There is dispute about what happened next. Choquette remembers that he had already seen the press reports on Tuesday morning and he wasn't surprised to hear from the APLQ and the MDPPQ. He says he phoned Maurice St. Pierre, the director-general of the QPF, to see if provincial policemen were involved. According to Choquette, St. Pierre got back to him later and said there was nothing to it. St. Pierre denies that he ever spoke to Choquette about the matter. He says he never got the phone call nor reported to the minister that police weren't involved.

In any event, Choquette wrote back to the APLQ and the MDPPQ, informing them that no police were involved from any force and that the Montreal police were carrying out their investigation. Choquette's reply was reported in the press and that ended the matter for the reporters and news editors.

A third APLQ-MDPPQ telegram was sent to federal Solicitor-General Goyer. His aide, J.R. Cameron, fired it off to RCMP Commissioner W.L. Higgitt for the force to draft a reply. Cameron's transfer note was marked urgent because the APLQ and the MDPPQ wanted a reply by Friday. Two weeks later the Mounties came back with a recommendation that no reponse should be made. And none was.

At G-section in Montreal, Vermette and Cobb knew that they would have to report Operation Bricole to headquarters because of the initial press reports that Tuesday morning. In the communications room at RCMP headquarters on Alta Vista Drive in Ottawa a Telex machine began to clatter with an "urgent—top secret" message addressed personally to Director-General Starnes. Starnes was told that in regard to the press reports, Security Service men in Montreal participated in a joint operation with the other two forces. "There were no difficulties and the operation was a success." The message erroneously reported that the documents were being held by the Montreal police.

John Starnes was furious. Starnes was a diplomat and a bureaucrat by training and inclination. Although he had worked in military intelligence during World War II, most of his government service had been in the diplomatic corps. He wasn't a policeman and he never pretended to be. But he excelled as an administrator. Because Starnes had become the first civilian head of the Security Service, many of the old timers at headquarters couldn't bring themselves to fully trust him—a man who had never gone through the initiation rites at the Regina training depot and had never served in the ranks. But Starnes thought he had a good working relationship with Cobb. He liked the younger man. When he was in Ottawa, Cobb would regularly call on Starnes and the two would have long, rambling philosophical discussions about the role of an intelligence agency. Cobb would sometimes argue that the director-general should be protected from knowledge of shady operations in the field so that the chief could honestly deny he knew what was going on if the roof caved in, leaving a lower-ranking officer to catch the flak. Starnes had rejected that idea and now he was presented with just such a problem. He scrawled across the bottom of the Telex, "I find it difficult to understand why I or my senior colleagues were not advised of this delicate joint operation in advance and especially in this pre-election atmosphere."

During the next two days the men in G-section in Montreal monitored the cobra wiretap carefully. From it they learned that members of the APLQ and the MDPPQ had no evidence that police were responsible for the wiretap. The radicals were only guessing and they were worried that compromising documents might have been taken.

By Thursday Cameron's "urgent" note to Higgitt landed on a desk at Alta Vista Drive. It was a time for explanations and there was a flurry of top secret Telex exchanges between Ottawa and Montreal all day long. Vermette's first response was to try to minimize Security Service involvement. He said that Operation Bricole was planned by Cormier of the Montreal police and that the operation was under that force's control. There was also a considerable effort to reassure Ottawa that a secure cover-up was in place. Vermette explained that no fingerprints were left and that the documents were being kept in a "safe house" under tight guard. The message didn't mention that the "safe house" was Sergeant Brodeur's basement and that security was provided by Mrs. Brodeur and the family's Doberman pinscher. "No damage was done to the premises and precautions were taken that no fingerprints or other clues would be left on the premises," the Telex said.

Starnes was worried about keeping the lid on too. He Telexed back: "You will not be surprised that I was considerably irritated to learn, after the fact, of the operation . . . and particularly since I made it clear to Inspector Cobb when he was here last week that I felt headquarters should be informed in advance of such actions in this pre-election situation." Starnes asked for more details "in order to decide how best to deal with the matter in terms of the prime minister and the minister." He scolded the Montreal men for their shortsightedness. "Since it must have been obvious to all those concerned that representations of this kind (the telegrams from the MDPPQ and the APLQ to Goyer) would be made, I was equally irritated to discover only today that the three police forces met yesterday to see if they could agree on a common line in recommending the kind of response which should be made to these representations. . . ." (The three forces decided to stonewall it and ignore the telegrams.)

Starnes continued, "Needless to say, had I known about the proposed action in advance I would have strongly recommended in this pre-election period that the RCMP not involve itself. In the circumstances I sincerely hope that the Sûreté [QPF] and the Montreal city police are agreed on the need to make no use whatever of material they may have acquired through the operation which can lead to public controversy and that knowledge of it will be limited to the fewest number of persons possible." Starnes failed to express any concern that the break-in had been conducted without a search warrant and that it might be illegal.

Vermette responded with repeated assurances that Bricole had been primarily a Montreal police operation "because of territorial jurisdiction," but he acknowledged that Mounties had been in on the planning. He failed to mention that he had agreed to the plan in principle.

Meanwhile, strange things were happening in Sergeant Brodeur's basement. He didn't go downstairs because his end of the operation was complete. The old "need-to-know" principle was at work. But throughout the week Mrs. Brodeur played hostess to a number of policemen who arrived each morning to sort through the documents. The sorting was done by members of all three forces, including Samson and Marie-Claire Dubé, a young civilian intelligence analyst from G-section.

Dubé, a psychology graduate from Loyola University, was the kind of person who didn't ask too many questions. She knew how tight-lipped the Mounties could be about their work. Her father, Yves Dubé, was a high-ranking officer with the force and she herself later married a Mountie. She didn't know where the documents came from but was bright enough to figure out that she was probably sorting through stolen material. Her suspicions were aroused by the unusual circumstances—working in someone's basement—and by the strange way the men were behaving. Samson was flitting around the basement with his new Minox mini-camera, snapping pictures of people sorting through the documents. An officer from one of the other forces protested angrily and Samson stopped. (The negatives disappeared mysteriously two years later when Samson was arrested on a bombing charge and his house was searched.)

The job of cataloguing the documents was slow and dull. There was a lot of duplicate material, such as back issues of the *Bulletin* and pamphlets. The duplicate documents were sorted into three piles—one for each force. One of the men found the Cossette-Trudel letter to Vandelac and showed it to Dubé. Everyone seemed to be excited by the find.

It was a long letter and it took about fifteen minutes to read. As a piece of intelligence, the letter turned out to be a great disappointment. It contained no secret plans for future terrorist acts. It contained no espionage codes. It contained no call for armed revolution. Instead, Jacques Cossette-Trudel wrote that he and his wife, Louise, were homesick for Quebec and that life in Cuba was pretty miserable. He confessed his deep shame for his part in the

Cross kidnapping and that he realized that terrorism was coun-
terproductive for the separatist movement. "The FLQ must disappear as a strategy ... we must stop terrorism. It's a double-edged
sword that was starting to cut off the heads of Québécois," he
wrote.

Some of the rambling Marxist rhetoric remained, but Cossette-
Trudel's new views closely paralleled those of Pierre Vallières,
once the FLQ's chief theoretician, who had come to renounce violence at just about the same time.

The policemen headed off to a post office to find a photocopy
machine. Copies of the letter were made—one for each force—
and the "safe house" operations were shut down. The Brodeur's
got their basement back and Mrs. Brodeur was given $35 a week
by the Mounties for her troubles. They had her sign a receipt in a
false name.

Two months later two bags full of documents from the break-
in were taken to headquarters in Ottawa. They were destroyed
sometime the following year.

Less than a month after the break-in Solicitor-General Goyer
met with RCMP Commissioner Higgitt and Director-General
Starnes. It was one of the first opportunities that the men had to
discuss the APLQ break-in. Whether in fact it was discussed is in
dispute. This was one of Goyer's last meetings with the senior
Mounties. He was moved to another portfolio in a post-election
cabinet shuffle. Goyer was certainly aware of the APLQ and the
break-in. The APLQ was on the list of current wiretaps and bugs
reviewed by Goyer at this meeting. He signed the review documents. The only other written documents from that meeting are
Higgitt's personal notes which he kept at home despite the fact
that they contained sensitive classified information. Higgitt's
notes show that five items were discussed, including a routine list
of officer promotions. But there is no mention in the notes of the
APLQ affair. Goyer denies that he ever asked Higgitt and Starnes
whether their men were responsible for the break-in. Rather
naively, Goyer thought it couldn't possibly be true. The Mounties
wouldn't break the law. But as Cobb himself told the McDonald
Commission, in the Security Service "we accept some things as
routine to the point that we don't think of them as illegal.... In

the security field laws seem less important than in the criminal field. This is a myth, of course, but it is accepted. . . . We should, if possible, act within the law. But if the law doesn't permit us to take the necessary steps we consider violating [it]. . . ."

Goyer had seen a press report in which Quebec Justice Minister Choquette, a personal acquaintance of his, denied that any police force was involved. As far as Goyer was concerned, that settled it and the question went unasked.

Higgitt and Starnes have a different version of that meeting. They say they entered the meeting fully intending to tell Goyer and they would be greatly surprised if they hadn't. Higgitt says it was "almost certain that the discussion did in fact take place."

Whether it did or it didn't, the result was that a cover-up successfully continued for three and a half years until, as Cobb feared, somebody talked.

3

Dirty Tricks

The APLQ break-in wasn't the first of the Security Service's dirty tricks. During 1971 and the early part of 1972 the men of G-section in Montreal burned a barn, stole a case of dynamite and a box of blasting caps and issued a fake Front de Libération du Québec terrorist communiqué. All this was done in the name of national security.

The October Crisis of 1970 shocked Canadians. And while it appeared to break the back of the terrorist fringe elements in Quebec, it also showed many Québécois that the federal government wouldn't hesitate to use all the powers of the state to attack separatism. The War Measures Act invoked by the federal cabinet suspended civil liberties. Hundreds of Québécois were rounded up in the night and held by police without being charged. The crisis passed, the Cross kidnappers were exiled to Cuba and the Laporte killers were arrested, tried and sent to prison. Young, radical separatists saw that their best hope rested with lawful, democratic means. The strength of the Parti Québécois grew as the FLQ began to disappear. The shooting war was over and separatists began to organize to win the peace, lawfully and peacefully. The Security Service didn't see it that way.

The police had been given unprecedented search, seizure and detention powers during the crisis. The legal formalities of arrest and search warrants weren't needed as long as the War Measures Act was in force. The police had enjoyed great freedom of action and it was difficult to go back to conventional ways. G-section, the Quebec anti-separatist unit, and other units in other forces hadn't been all that successful during the crisis even with their additional powers. Although the FLQ kidnappers and killers had been known to the police, it had been difficult to track them down and to discover their hideouts. The conclusion reached in Ottawa and in Montreal was that the Security Service should engage in offensive disruptive tactics rather than sit back to react when trouble developed. Field-unit commanders, such as Inspector Cobb in Montreal, felt they had been given a freer hand.

John Starnes, the director-general of the Security Service, wanted his men to be far more aggressive in their approach to separatist groups. In February 1971 headquarters devised a "counterterrorist program" that had as one of its essential elements plans for "disruption" of separatist groups. The concern was that it would take too long to successfully infiltrate such groups and in the short term dirty tricks would thwart separatist plans. The program was further refined five months later with a policy document dealing with "disruptive tactics" to cause "dissension and splintering of the separatist/terrorist groups."

In 1972, shortly before the barn burning and dynamite theft, Starnes told field commanders that he wanted the men to become "far more vigorous in their approach to disruptive activity." Men who balked at these approaches were to be censured "and if necessary, transfer" might be in order. Starnes claimed later that he didn't know G-section's dirty tricks went as far as the arson, dynamite theft and the issuing of the fake FLQ communiqué.

The Security Service's disruptive tactics program was essentially the same strategy employed in the United States by the FBI. The FBI's "counterintelligence program" (COINTELPRO) was used to disrupt the Communist party, civil rights groups, antiwar groups and the Ku Klux Klan from 1956 to 1971. It included attempts to harass and discredit civil rights leader Martin Luther King, Jr., and to intimidate him with the threat of releasing embarrassing tape recordings made in bugged hotel rooms.

The RCMP's disruptive tactics were to make use "of sophisticated and well-researched plans built around existing situations such as power struggles, love affairs" and other inside information that could be used to coerce or compromise individuals, an internal memo says. Incriminating information might include medical data showing that an individual had been treated by a psychiatrist. These kinds of dirty tricks weren't confined to Quebec. They were employed against New Left and socialist groups in Ontario and elsewhere. Insp. Patrick Banning, one of the architects of the headquarter's plan for Quebec, said that disruption wasn't anything new for the Security Service. "You can refer to the Bible. We are the second oldest profession. . . . Delilah used a bit of a disruptive tactic against Samson."

G-section was beefed up. The nucleus remained the many old hands from D-section, the general anti-terrorist and anti-subversive squad. But a special capability was needed for G-section in Quebec. The prime requirement was a cadre of francophone Mounties. The duty rosters of Quebec and New Brunswick were scoured for new recruits for G-section. The younger men were green. But they were eager to perform national security work.

Disturbing rumours circulated in Quebec City and Montreal as the first anniversary of the October Crisis approached. The word on the street was that the FLQ was going to try again. The rumours were hard to pin down. The Security Service had few reliable informers. Yet Cobb and the others knew that they would be remiss if they didn't pursue their meagre leads.

The most visible signs of the terrorist threat were the periodic appearance of communiqués issued by anonymous people claiming to be the remaining forces of the Front de Libération du Québec. Reporters were the most frequent recipients of the communiqués. The journalists couldn't ignore the possibility that they were real. Police also took them seriously. It later turned out that many of the communiqués were written by young pranksters with a sick sense of humour or by slightly deranged individuals who saw a chance for a secret moment of importance by claiming to be FLQ. The Security Service learned that just about anyone could put his political thoughts to paper and get some attention by signing it FLQ.

But patterns began to emerge. The Security Service believed

there was something to be seriously concerned about in the communiqués issued in the name of the cell La Minerve, the name of a nineteenth-century Montreal French-language news-paper. During the first October Crisis anniversary period two La Minerve communiqués appeared. They described the anniversary as "Liberation-Phase II."

The communiqués had an obvious Marxist tone. The first urged that "working people arise" and promised that the FLQ was "ready for action" to lead the Québécois to independence from Ottawa and from capitalism. But the chief target of the writer's venom was Quebec Premier Robert Bourassa. Many Québécois, including staunch federalists, thought that Bourassa had abdicated his leadership role to Ottawa during the October Crisis. Bourassa was seen as the weak puppet of Prime Minister Trudeau. The communiqué played upon this theme. "The nigger king Bourassa will get what he deserves... nobody can stop the revolution."

The second La Minerve communiqué was even more frightening. It contained a death threat for Bourassa. "Robert, make your will. Soon you will rejoin the one you so cowardly abandoned," a reference to the murdered Pierre Laporte.

Bourassa was under regular and tight bodyguard protection by the QPF throughout his term. The threats in the communiqués didn't prompt any increased security.

The communiqués were studied and analysed by G-section and passed along to headquarters for further study. The handwriting was examined. The use of phrases was compared to previous communiqués. Reporters who received the communiqués were questioned about the voices of the anonymous callers who had said where the documents could be found. Authorship was never determined.

But this scare, coupled with the other street rumours, kept the Security Service on a war footing during the month of October. Street contacts and informers were questioned again and again. Yet October passed without incident.

November was uneventful. Then in December a voice from the past was heard from again. Pierre Vallières, whose book, *White Niggers of America*, had stirred separatist passions during the

1960s, had been in hiding. He had been considered the most influential separatist intellectual of his time. On December 13 Vallières wrote to *Le Devoir*, the respected French-language Montreal daily edited by Claude Ryan. It was a long letter reviewing the history of the separatist movement and examining its failings during the October Crisis. Most importantly, Vallières called for separatists to abandon violence and join the democratic Parti Québécois. Independence was to be won at the polling booth, not in the underground hideouts of the FLQ.

Cobb was cynical. He didn't believe that Vallières was sincere. He thought it was a trick and that the Parti Québécois would be used as a cover for the FLQ. Terrorism would surface again at a more opportune moment. Nevertheless, Vallières' new manifesto had a profound effect on intellectual life in the province. While Cobb stewed, most others breathed a sigh of relief and believed that normalcy had returned at last.

Two weeks later phones rang in several newsrooms in Montreal and Quebec City. The anonymous callers said they were from the FLQ. There was a new and important communiqué to be found. In Montreal reporters followed instructions and hurried off to a washroom at one of Quebec's most important religious shrines, St. Joseph's Oratory. As promised, there they found copies of a handwritten communiqué with the now familiar rough sketch of a pipe-smoking habitant with a rifle in his hands. The communiqué was signed La Minerve cell of the FLQ.

If there had been reason to believe that Vallières' new manifesto had marked the end of a turbulent era, this new communiqué seemed to be trying to shatter that. The communiqué denounced Vallières as a traitor to the revolution and a coward. Vallières, it said, "can only write words." His "new ideas" of joining ranks with the Parti Québécois must be rejected. The PQ was made up of the petit bourgeois. René Lévesque and company were accomplices "of the fascists in authority." There were references to violence. "What good is it to infiltrate the PQ when we can arrive at our goals by our own arms?" The communiqué said that the FLQ was the only force fighting the exploiters of the proletariat. And in case anyone had missed the point, it added, "Mao, the true revolutionary, teaches us that power flows from the barrel of a gun."

The communiqué got wide publicity, including a mention in *Time* magazine. Police took it seriously. Copies of this third communiqué, like the other two, were passed along to Security Service headquarters. Solicitor-General Goyer was advised of this latest development and was told that it appeared there was still an active FLQ. The analysts noted that the handwriting was different from the first two. But the style of writing was the same. It seemed that there was still cause to worry. Moreover there were no clues regarding the identities of the members of the La Minerve cell.

The identity of the author of the third communiqué remained a secret for six years. It was written by Inspector Cobb.

Cobb had some assistance. Hélène Vigeant, a civilian member of the force, was a linguist and she helped with the terminology to make sure Cobb got it right. A Security Service member with some artistic talent did the sketch of the habitant. Two of Cobb's men— Sgt. Bernard Dubuc and Const. Richard Daigle— distributed the communiqués for the journalists to find. But the idea was Cobb's alone. The message was his. He never reported to his superiors that the third communiqué was a fake that he had written.

The idea came to Cobb as he mulled over Vallières' letter to *Le Devoir*. There was a danger, he thought, if violence-prone felquistes (FLQ members) infiltrated the PQ. For one thing, it would be harder to keep track of them if they were no longer isolated from the political mainstream. As a federal policeman he didn't have much respect for the separatist goals of the PQ, but since it was a democratic party it deserved police protection from infiltrators. "It was important to try to confuse the situation and dissuade them from joining the PQ," he told the McDonald Commission. The RCMP "has a duty to protect that institution." The idea of trying to sow confusion grew in Cobb's mind. He wanted to try to control events to prevent felquistes from joining the PQ. Cobb saw his "duty" and he sat down with a piece of paper.

He thought carefully. He didn't want to repeat any of the death threats against Bourassa. "There was no intention of inciting violence." Yet he wanted the communiqué to appear and sound as authentic as possible. He tried to get the proper Marxist tone with the right catch phrases: "The medium was the message," he said. By discrediting Vallières he hoped the message would convince some to remain loyal to the teachings of Charles Gagnon, an early FLQ figure who advocated a workers' party.

When Cobb had finished he thought he had what he called a satisfactory piece of "disinformation"—a classic intelligence service technique "to create confusion in the milieu as to what course people should take" so that they end up doing nothing. Cobb would have to be naive not to recognize that once "disinformation" gets out all kinds of people may in fact do something about it. Other policemen might spend a lot of time and effort tracking down its source. A crazed individual might try to go out and find power with the barrel of a gun. Or a communiqué of this sort might be just the last straw an uptight Westmount anglophone might need to pack up his family and head for Toronto.

Cobb testified that if the situation got out of hand he would have confessed his authorship. Yet he seemed bitter about the fact that one of his former subordinates, Donald McCleery, eventually tipped Deputy Solicitor-General Roger Tasse to G-section's dirty tricks. "You can't trust anyone to keep anything secret. Maybe you shouldn't," Cobb said.

Cobb got a chuckle out of the idea of newsmen treating the communiqué as legitimate. Quebec journalists had not always cooperated fully with the Security Service in investigations of separatists' movements. Now the journalists were the unwitting accomplices in a Security Service operation. It was poetic justice, he thought.

The barn burning incident was Staff Sgt. Donald McCleery's own way to employ disruptive tactics to try to control events. That was his method of making sure an FLQ meeting wouldn't take place. Cobb might tinker with Marxist rhetoric, but McCleery preferred his own direct approach to a problem. He didn't have much time for Cobb's organizational charts and fancy theories. McCleery was blunt. McCleery and his men had worked around the clock during the October Crisis while Cobb was away studying at university. A bond had formed among the men who were in on the big operation. Those who weren't part of it were never a part of the group. Like Cobb, McCleery worked as an office clerk after high school. He joined the force at nineteen in 1953.

The Security Service had been interested in a farm near Ste-Anne-de-la-Rochelle for some time. It was located in an out-of-the-way corner of the Eastern Townships, about fifty miles southeast of Montreal near the United States border. It was owned by relatives of FLQ kidnappers Jacques and Paul Rose. The Mounties thought it could be used as a hideout. A group of generally peaceful leftist intellectuals and union organizers had other plans for it. It was called La Grange du Petit Québec Libre. The farm and its buildings were to be used as a kind of community centre and weekend retreat for artists, poets, musicians and their families. The musicians of Jazz Libre du Québec were to perform there. The plans were hardly a secret. They were given favourable publicity in March 1971 in *Perspective* magazine, a weekend French-language newspaper supplement.

In the spring of 1972 McCleery felt he had good intelligence information that the farm was to be used as a meeting place for members of the FLQ and Black Panthers from south of the border. There was a fear that the militant Black Panthers might use the meeting as a training session for FLQ members in the use of firearms and explosives. McCleery wanted to know what was happening at the meeting. But it was to be held in the barn, an isolated building where it would be difficult to plant bugs. McCleery felt he had to stop the meeting before it took place or to force it to be held somewhere else where the Security Service would have a better chance of bugging it. He didn't think there was any alternative but to burn the barn down.

"Don't get the idea we were a bunch of hoodlums running around burning down barns," McCleery later testified. "I was in the Security Service twenty years and there was only one barn burned."

Desperate situations require desperate measures, he thought. The FLQ wasn't a bunch of choirboys or boy scouts. They didn't ask for warrants to plant bombs, he said later. So McCleery put the Security Service into the same category. He didn't ask for a search warrant to check out the meeting to see if small arms training was really being conducted. McCleery remembers, however, that he told Cobb of the plan to burn the barn. Cobb denies this.

Sometime during the first week of May, McCleery assigned the task to Cpl. Bernard Dubuc and Const. Richard Daigle. Daigle was a relative newcomer to G-section and had spent his first six months reading G-section files. He didn't have a lot of experience in operations. But he had just recently received a higher security classification and was initiated into some of the darker secrets of the service. He learned of puma and vampire operations, code names for break-ins. But setting fire to a barn seemed to be a lot different. Dubuc, the more experienced hand, told Daigle that if they had orders from McCleery he shouldn't worry. It must be an approved operation. The way to get ahead was to participate in clandestine operations, Dubuc explained.

Dubuc and Daigle set out in an unmarked car for some preliminary reconnaissance patrols. They were going to case the farm to see how the barn might be approached at night without the men being spotted. Neither man was familiar with the backroads in the Ste-Anne area and they had problems. On the second patrol Dubuc drove the car over a large rock on one of the backroads. The engine's oil pan broke and the men had to get a tow truck to tow them back to Montreal. That kind of bad luck continued to plague the operation.

McCleery wasn't pleased with the progress of his amateur arsonists. He assigned a third member to the torch team. McCleery took Cpl. Claude Brodeur aside in the office and asked him to give Dubuc and Daigle a hand with a delicate operation at the leftists' farm. Brodeur was assigned because he knew the area well. He'd grown up near Ste-Anne and he had travelled the backroads on a bike as a kid. Brodeur was curious. He asked McCleery what Daigle and Dubuc were up to. "They're going to burn the fucking joint," McCleery replied coolly.

The day of the operation Dubuc decided a fourth man was needed to stay with the getaway car. He approached Cpl. Bernard Blier who went along for the ride. Dubuc had told him that he was needed to mind the car while the others went on a sneak scouting trip. Blier can't remember ever being told the mission was arson. His thoughts were elsewhere that day. He was having marital problems—his wife had just left him and their two small girls.

The afternoon of the operation Dubuc checked the weather forecast. He was pleased. He wanted a calm night so that there wouldn't be any wind to spread the fire. And there had been some recent rainfall near Ste-Anne, enough moisture to keep the ground damp and prevent a field fire. The forecast looked good. Late in the afternoon the men left the Security Service offices on St. Catherine Street and piled their bulky frames into a beat-up eight-year-old unmarked RCMP car. They headed out to the suburbs of Ville LaSalle and Longueuil where they stopped at each of their homes to change into old clothes. There was still plenty of daylight as they started towards Ste-Anne, and lots of time to take a short detour to stop and inspect a small country lot owned by Brodeur. There was another stop for apples.

Blier and Dubuc got hungry for some dinner. The men pulled into a roadside canteen, one of Quebec's familiar chip stands, to get a bite to eat. Blier had two or three hot dogs. Dubuc had a hot dog and a hamburger. Since there was still more time to kill before nightfall, the men drove into Granby and stopped at a hotel tavern. Blier started to feel nauseous from the hot dogs. He ordered a ginger ale and nursed his stomach during the conversation. Daigle had a mug of draft beer. Dubuc had two or three beers. Brodeur, the guide, didn't drink.

As they sat in the tavern, Dubuc, Daigle and Brodeur talked about their plans to set the fire. Blier was in a daze for most of the rest of the night and he can't remember the conversation at all. He was feeling too ill and on top of that he was thinking about his marriage problems.

By the time they left the hotel it had begun to rain heavily. In the close confines of the car Blier thought he was going to vomit. They stopped the car several times for Blier to catch some air. Through the heavy rain the men continued. Brodeur guided them along back roads and at about midnight they reached a safe, hidden location on a gravel road which ran parallel to the farm. They were about two miles from the barn and the farmhouse. Blier stayed in the car while the others got out and went around to the trunk to get a can of oil. The men have conflicting recollections of whether it was motor oil or stove oil.

Dubuc, Daigle and Brodeur left Blier and headed off through

the bush and swampy fields. They reached the area of the barn in about thirty minutes. They watched for awhile. There were no lights in the farmhouse and it appeared that there was nobody around. Dubuc stayed back a bit to serve as lookout while Daigle and Brodeur entered the barn. It was a large building, perhaps thirty feet high. There were many large cracks between the wooden wall boards. Part of the floor was dirt and part was a cement pad that might have been used to park a tractor or car. Brodeur spread a quart of oil on the cement. Daigle, the rookie, thought it was strange to try to burn cement. But he didn't say anything. It took Brodeur several matches to get the oil to ignite. When it started, however, it threw off a lot of heat, smoke and flame. Brodeur and Daigle got out.

Dubuc and Daigle thought the barn was about to go up in a blaze. They sprinted back to the car as quickly as they could. Brodeur lingered at a distance, waiting for the wooden structure to catch fire. He waited for about ten minutes. The fire went out. Brodeur wasn't about to go back to the barn alone. He trudged back to the car to give his partners the bad news.

When Dubuc and Daigle got to the car they found that Blier was still in pain. But they had a more serious concern. The car wouldn't start. They tinkered under the hood for awhile and had the engine going by the time Brodeur caught up with them.

The men realized they were in a spot. They were stuck out in the middle of nowhere on a rainy night with an unreliable car. They had a partner who might be suffering from food poisoning and might throw up at any minute. And what was worse, they had failed to carry out McCleery's orders to "burn the fucking joint."

The first concern was the getaway car. While they still could, they drove the twenty miles to the nearby town of Magog. They hunted without luck for an all-night garage. Brodeur, however, knew someone in Magog who might help—a man who had once acted as an informer. They drove to the man's house and woke him up. Once more the man was asked to help the Mounties on a secret mission. They didn't tell him what it was all about, but the man loaned them his truck. All four Mounties crammed themselves into the cab of the half-ton pickup. Brodeur drove. Blier sat partially on Dubuc's lap and partially on Daigle's and complained of more nausea. On the way back to the farm Brodeur made a stop for Blier who at last threw up at the side of the road.

At the previous hiding spot Brodeur pulled the truck over to the side. He and Daigle got out and headed once more across the fields with their second quart of oil. Dubuc was tired and he stayed behind with Blier. For the second time that night Brodeur poured oil in the barn and set it afire. The fire caught this time and the barn was soon ablaze. The two men ran back to the truck. With his heart pounding and while he tried to catch his wind, Daigle thought he heard a dog barking in the distance. The two men were exhausted when they reached the truck. Blier was asleep. It was about 4 a.m. and the men were anxious to get back to Montreal. As they drove off Daigle caught a glimpse of a fiery sky, but it seemed it might have been only a dream.

They returned the truck to Magog and tried to start their own car again. It wouldn't work. The men debated whether to spend the night with Brodeur's friend or to try to find another way back to Montreal before dawn. Brodeur wanted the men back in the office in the morning so that questions wouldn't be raised. Dubuc fiddled under the hood for awhile and got the car started. They made it home in time to shower, shave and report to the office.

The men of G-section worked in an open-concept plan office which was designed to facilitate the exchange of ideas, a step that Cobb encouraged with his regular morning section meetings. But the "need-to-know" principle of secrecy prevailed. G-section members were so secretive about their tasks that if they were working on sensitive files at their desks they would close them up and cover their work when a colleague approached.

Daigle ran into McCleery in the hallway that day. "Everything went well? No problems?" McCleery asked. The weary rookie just nodded his head yes. The "need-to-know" principle prevented the four men from discussing their triumph with anyone other than McCleery. There were no written reports. They couldn't file expense accounts for the purchase of the oil.

A few mornings later at a general meeting of the section a Quebec Police Force intelligence report about La Grange was mentioned. It just so happened that a mysterious fire had destroyed the barn. There were some knowing smirks, but nobody said anything. The QPF had tried to inspect the debris, but the owners chased the provincial police away. A few weeks later the charred site was bulldozed over by the owners.

Dubuc and Daigle were teamed together on another bizarre assignment in the spring of 1972. Their job was to steal explosives. Dubuc says he got the orders from McCleery. McCleery denies this. What's more, if he were to send anyone on a job like that it wouldn't have been this pair because there were others "who were a lot more crackerjack than those two guys."

The motives for the theft are just as mysterious. Dubuc says McCleery told him that the dynamite was needed to give to an informer so that he could establish credibility with a terrorist cell. Daigle says that's the same story he got from Dubuc at the time. A third participant in the heist, Cpl. Normand Chamberland, has given two different stories about what it was all about. During an internal RCMP investigation in 1977 he said Dubuc and Daigle thought the dynamite might be planted in the home of an alleged Montreal terrorist. He said later, however, that his memory had been off and the plan was just to scare the alleged terrorist by making him think that his fingerprints were on the dynamite. But, he says, the plan was too weird to carry out.

There's not any agreement on when the dynamite was taken or even how much was taken. Dubuc and Daigle say it was in late May after the barn fire. Official records from the company that lost the explosives and a theft report to the dangerous explosives branch of the Department of Energy, Mines and Resources suggest that the theft was a month earlier, in April. Dubuc says one case of dynamite was taken from one building and a box of detonators from a second building. Daigle can only remember the dynamite. The company's records show that four cases of dynamite and one hundred blasting caps were stolen.

Even the facts that aren't in dispute have an element of incredibility. One day in the Security Service office Dubuc told young Daigle that the two of them had an important mission. They were to find explosives for McCleery. Neither man had the faintest clue as to how to obtain dynamite. They thought about the possibility of going to a store to buy it. They didn't know what procedures were required. Without identifying themselves they phoned a rural detachment of the RCMP and were told to come to the detachment office to fill out the proper government forms, stating the reason they wanted dynamite and how much they intended to purchase. That was a totally unsatisfactory procedure. This was, after all, a clandestine national security operation. It began to dawn on the men that they would have to do something else.

They had heard stories from time to time about how kids found sticks of dynamite lying around construction sites. They too might be as lucky. For two weeks Daigle and Dubuc drove around the countryside of the Eastern Townships in search of construction sites. It was a pleasant enough way to pass the time and a welcome break from files, paperwork and office work. But they had no luck finding dynamite.

Then one day back in the office Dubuc overheard a colleague tell another member of the Security Service that it was such a shame that the police worked so hard to stop bombings "when places like Richelieu Construction leave explosives sitting around." Dubuc didn't ask any questions. He rounded up Daigle and the two went off to find the Richelieu site. They got the address, a location near Iberville in the Eastern Townships. They drove to the site and spotted signs posted on sheds that explosives were stored inside. The sheds were in an isolated field near a high cliff. There were no fences. It looked like an ideal place for a break-in.

When they got back to Montreal they got Corporal Chamberland to help out. They didn't tell Chamberland what it was about. But they needed him to stay with the getaway car. Late that night they set out in an old, unmarked car. Chamberland gathered from the conversation of the other two men that the assignment had something to do with explosives and it probably involved theft. He wasn't worried about the legality because Dubuc and Daigle must be acting under orders.

The men figured that a parked car near the site would be too suspicious. Chamberland dropped off his passengers and set a pick-up time for later. Dubuc and Daigle made their way by flashlight to a shed. Dubuc carried a tire iron and used it to snap the combination padlock. He reached inside, dragged a forty-pound case of dynamite across the floor to the door and gave it to Daigle to carry to the pick-up point. At 2 a.m. Chamberland returned on schedule. The dynamite was put in the trunk and Dubuc put the detonator caps in the glove compartment. Dubuc drove the other men home. He kept the car for the night. Dubuc was worried about carting around high explosives. One stick of the dynamite had enough explosive force to reduce three cubic yards of solid rock to dust and rubble. There were fourteen sticks in one case. Dubuc didn't want to park the car in his garage. He left it in a shopping centre parking lot near his home in Ville LaSalle.

The next morning in the office Dubuc told Daigle that McCleery had offered to store the dynamite at his summer cottage near St-Faustin in the Laurentians. McCleery had given Dubuc keys to the summer place and remembers allowing the dynamite to be stored at his cottage. But he says Dubuc told him the explosives came from an informer who got cold feet and wouldn't use them to gain credibility with a terrorist cell. McCleery thinks the dynamite might have been sitting under a desk in the office for some time before it was taken to his cottage.

Dubuc drove the car with the dynamite in the trunk. He was worried about a possible rear-end collision in busy downtown Montreal traffic. Daigle was assigned to drive a backup car to prevent anyone from hitting Dubuc's car. Off they went to the cottage. The men got back later that afternoon for Dubuc's going-away party. He was being transferred to another city.

When summer arrived McCleery's family planned to use the cottage. He didn't want the dynamite sitting around. It had to be moved again. McCleery says that he and Claude Brodeur took it away to another cottage site near Rougemont and buried it there. Brodeur says the dynamite was taken to an abandoned cabin near the U.S. border.

Sometime that fall, probably around October, Brodeur approached Daigle and told him that the dynamite had to be disposed of. Daigle helped move the deteriorating case of dynamite to a rural roadside. Moisture had caused the deterioration. Daigle remembered hearing somewhere that deteriorating dynamite was especially volatile. His last task in the operation was to place an anonymous phone call to the QPF to tell them where the cache of dynamite could be found.

Disruptive tactics were encouraged from the top. Commissioner Higgitt and Director-General Starnes were to claim later that they never knew that these "excesses" of G-section had taken place. But once any intelligence agency moves from the reactive and passive role to an aggressive and offensive position the argument becomes one of merely where to draw the line. In the fake communiqué case the Security Service was trying to control political events in Quebec. Political history has shown, in Israel for example, that yesterday's terrorist can become today's statesman. If indeed FLQ members or sympathizers were joining a legitimate democratic movement, that intelligence information should have been a cause for rejoicing. The barn burning was an attempt to stop a meeting that might have been totally innocent. The excuse that it was impossible to bug the barn doesn't hold water when one considers that twice G-section members were able to enter the structure clandestinely to try to set it ablaze. The dynamite theft, well, who knows what that was really about? But it's clear that G-section's disruptive tactics were dangerous police interference with the political and property rights of citizens.

4

Informers

On Monday, October 5, 1970, armed men forced British Trade Commissioner James Cross into a car and drove him away. This was the first of a series of incidents which came to be known as the October Crisis. Almost exactly one year later a similar scene was repeated on a Montreal street. The men responsible were not members of the Front de Libération du Québec. They were from the RCMP Security Service.

Paul Doucet* had no reason to believe anything unusual would happen to him on Monday, October 4, 1971. He had an appointment that morning with officials from the Unemployment Insurance Commission. He was collecting UIC benefits and there seemed to be some misunderstanding. He left his apartment and drove to the UIC offices in downtown Montreal. There he was told that UIC had the information that he was working while he collected UIC. He explained that wasn't the case, cleared up the

---

*This name is fictitious. The names of all civilians in this chapter have been changed. Some have criminal records and have long since paid for their crimes. Others appear to have been the innocent victims of circumstance. Most told their stories in public testimony and were subjected to cross-examination by lawyers for the RCMP who were attempting to discredit these witnesses' accounts. Their past activities and associations were not the subject of the public inquiries and there is no purpose to be served by identifying them again in this book.

matter and left.

Doucet's situation was like that of many other young Montrealers in their twenties. He was out of work and looking for a job. He had been mildly interested in politics and he had a few friends who were active in the separatist movement. In the late Sixties Doucet had been a member of a local riding executive for the Rassemblement pour l'Indépendence Nationale, the forerunner of the Parti Québécois. He had been a volunteer for awhile with a group known as the St. Henri Neighbourhood Workers' Committee. The group's chief activity was to try to get a health clinic for poor people. He lost interest and dropped out after his wife found a lover in the group. Doucet had limited work skills. He had been a machine operator in a factory. He was not a deep political thinker, but he enjoyed listening to his friend, Marc Bouchard, discuss politics.

Doucet was driving a borrowed Plymouth Valiant on this morning. When he left the UIC offices he drove to Old Montreal for a luncheon engagement with a friend. At about 1:30 p.m. he left the restaurant alone and headed for a drive to Mount Royal. Unbeknownst to him, his every move had been observed.

As he headed north on Park Avenue and under a bridge he caught a glimpse of a car in his rearview mirror. The car pulled out and sped up to pass. As it swung in front of the Valiant a second car pulled alongside. A third car pulled up in back to close the gap behind the Valiant. Then suddenly the first car began to brake. And then the others. The Valiant was boxed in by cars on three sides. The trap was completed on the right by a concrete retaining wall. Doucet had no choice but to stop. The men in the three unmarked cars were policemen. They had been tailing Doucet and had kept in touch with each other with two-way radios. They timed and executed their interception well. Sgt. Laurent Hugo, a former insurance salesman, was the team leader. Hugo was the first man out of his car. He strode to the Valiant and identified himself to Doucet as a policeman. Doucet thought the men were from the Montreal police. He was puzzled and slightly shaken by this interception. He had never been arrested before and he didn't think he had done anything illegal. Yet he figured he might be in for some trouble because he was carrying a driver's license that had been borrowed.

Hugo was wearing his .38-calibre snub-nosed Smith and Wesson police revolver. He says the gun remained in its holster the whole day. Doucet recalls that Hugo had his gun drawn as he approached the Valiant. But the gun was never pointed at him. The policemen had no arrest warrant. Nor did they have any reason to believe that Doucet had committed a crime. Nor that he was about to commit a crime. It didn't matter. They had plans for him.

Doucet got out of the Valiant, put his hands on the car roof and was frisked. Hugo remembers "inviting" Doucet "in a firm tone" to come with the police. Doucet felt he didn't have any choice. He recalls Hugo calling him a "piece of shit" and ordering him to get into the backseat of one of the unmarked cars. The police vehicle was a two-door model. Hugo got into the backseat next to Doucet. To get out Doucet would have had to climb past Hugo or over the driver, Cpl. Bernard Dubuc. He decided to sit silently and await his fate.

Doucet thought he was being taken to a police station where he might learn what this was all about. Instead Dubuc drove aimlessly around the Island of Montreal. Hugo began asking strange questions about why Doucet was hanging around with terrorists. They drove around the city for about an hour, Hugo doing most of the talking. The policemen had a proposition they wanted to put to Doucet. Borrowing a line from *The Godfather*, the police were going to make him an offer he probably couldn't refuse. Dubuc then drove north out of the city along Highway 11. About twenty minutes out of town Dubuc stopped the car. The policemen got out and conferred briefly about their next move. They decided to take Doucet to a motel where they could talk more easily with the man. At about 3 p.m. Dubuc saw a likely spot. It was a cheap seven-dollar-a-night motel along an isolated stretch of the road. Dubuc went in to register and then the men took Doucet to the room.

Hugo and Dubuc remember the rest of the night as a not totally unpleasant experience. Doucet was their guest and they wanted to put him at ease. They told him that they weren't violent men and they weren't going to hurt him. They realized that Doucet wasn't likely to try to leave because a person being questioned by police will probably stay put. "They want to know what we have on them," Hugo explains. Doucet was pretty quiet during the first few hours. So Hugo and Dubuc continued to talk about terrorism and how the police needed help to try to stop political violence, how Doucet might be able to help them out and in turn how the police could think of nonviolent ways for Québécois to present their grievances to the government. The policemen hinted around about Doucet's miserable circumstances as an unemployed factory worker, suggesting that they had a way whereby he could improve his lot and do something useful for his country. There were never any threats stated or implied.

Doucet has a totally different recollection. It was a harsh interrogation. Hugo pulled out his gun again and told Doucet that "accidents can take place easily." Doucet tried to put on a brave front, but he was frightened. He was made to sit in a chair next to the radiator coils in the warm, stuffy motel room. As the night wore on he got hot and tired. He was allowed up only to go to the toilet and even then one of the policemen followed him into the bathroom. The policemen showed Doucet pictures of his friend, Marc Bouchard, and other people who they described as terrorists. They wanted to know what Bouchard and his circle of friends were up to. Doucet remained silent.

The hours dragged by. Hugo went out to the motel's coffee shop for some food. While Hugo was away, Doucet remained in his chair and seemed to be trying to catch a nap. Dubuc rested on the bed and kept a wary eye on him. In his police training Dubuc had picked up a little bit of psychology. He had read an article about human behaviour and the principles of communication. He had learned techniques of "ego inflation and ego deflation" and thought he might try some of the ego deflation on Doucet now. He shouted at Doucet to quit pretending that he was asleep. He cursed Doucet and told him to stand up and face the wall. Doucet complied.

Hugo walked into the room clutching a bag of food and a carton of soft drinks. He saw Doucet standing in the corner and told him to sit down and "quit acting like a child." The men offered Doucet some of the food but he was proud and stubborn and wouldn't take any. The hours passed. From time to time one of the policemen got up and went out for some fresh air or a coffee.

At one point the policemen said that if Doucet didn't start to talk they would take him to the police station. That was exactly what Doucet wanted. If he could get to a police station he might be able to win his freedom. Doucet began to doubt that the men were who they said they were. He didn't yet know what police force they were from. When asked to see some identification, Hugo pulled out an RCMP card with his picture and the maple leaf emblem on it.

Time passed slowly. It was about 3 a.m. and Doucet had been cooped up in the room for about twelve hours. He began to reason that the only way he was ever going to get out was to begin to play along and to answer the questions. He began to talk. He said that he had known Bouchard and his friends for some time, none of them were criminals, but they were separatists. Hugo slipped out of the room and phoned a staff sergeant to tell him they were having some success. The noncommissioned officer never did ask how the interrogation was being conducted.

Doucet was talking so much now that the police had to call a halt to it. They wanted him to get home to have some sleep before he met with Bouchard later in the day. They felt confident that they had won over a reliable informer. Dubuc and Hugo drove Doucet back to where the Valiant had been parked by another member of the interception team. They gave Doucet five dollars to buy some breakfast and had him sign a receipt. It was 7:15 a.m. — more than sixteen hours after he had been stopped — and Doucet felt he was free.

He met his friend Bouchard at lunchtime. Doucet was nervous but didn't tell his friend what had happened. He was uncomfortable and felt that he was being followed by someone. In fact, twenty-six members of a Security Service surveillance team kept track of Doucet's movements for the next twenty-four hours. On Wednesday, Doucet phoned Hugo at the RCMP to say he wasn't able to keep a scheduled rendezvouz with the Mounties that day, claiming to have to meet Bouchard at a discotheque instead. Hugo told him to keep the appointment with Bouchard and not to worry. If anything were to start to happen Doucet was to get down on the floor at the disco and stay there.

Doucet talked with Bouchard on the phone that day. The conversation was bugged. Doucet told Bouchard what had happened Monday night. He told of the interception and the questioning by the Mounties in the motel room. He embellished the story, telling Bouchard that the Mounties had tied him up while he was grilled. "I didn't intend to become a stool pigeon . . . a buddy's a buddy," Doucet said. He added to the story so that Bouchard might realize how much pressure he had been under. Bouchard was angry and told Doucet that he had foolishly set back the independence movement by twenty years. When the conversation was over, Doucet felt totally alone. He thought the Mounties were on to him and wanted him to become a stool pigeon. He didn't want to betray friends. He decided to drop from sight.

Doucet felt certain now that he was being tailed. He grabbed a taxi to a Metro station and then took the subway to Place du Canada in downtown Montreal. Along the way he lost the people tailing him. Doucet went to a farm owned by some of his other friends. He stayed there for a couple of months and then he moved to Quebec City. He was afraid to try to collect UIC or apply for any other social benefits because he felt the Mounties could trace his whereabouts. He wanted to be rid of the police once and for all. Doucet supported himself with odd jobs and handouts. He lived underground for a year, the life of a fugitive. Yet he was accused of no crime. He had done nothing except to be a friend to a man the police were suspicious of.

Bouchard also tried to drop from sight. He and a friend, Michel Lavoie, left Montreal and lived at another farm under assumed names. They weren't as successful as Doucet. The Security Service knew exactly where they were.

The men of G-section had failed badly in their first attempt to recruit an informer. Not only had they bungled the job of trying to get Doucet's cooperation, but in the process Bouchard and Lavoie, their prime terrorist suspects, were tipped off that the police were out for them. If the Mounties don't get their man they sometimes try for another. So it was with Louis Mercier who became G-section's second target for an informer recruitment attempt.

Mercier was a rather unsuccessful Montreal artist. He had a criminal record for terrorist activity but had served his time and wanted nothing more than to live in peace and tranquillity with his wife, his two cats and his paintings.

During the early 1960s Mercier had been a young student who was intrigued with the romance of revolution. He dreamed of an independent Quebec and he was impatient. He felt the road to independence was one of armed struggle. He and a few friends decided to take action. The young, naive idealists were doomed to failure. Armed with two hunting rifles, the friends staged a break-in and made off with some dynamite. Before they had a chance to use it they were arrested—within a matter of hours. In August 1964 Mercier and the others were convicted of possession of explosives, public mischief, forced entry, possession of guns and attempted armed robbery. Mercier spent four years in prison. The revolutionary dream still held him in its grip. On the outside, in 1968, he and two friends headed out for Mexico. From there they planned to go to Cuba to harvest sugar cane. But in Mexico Mercier had what he describes as a spiritual experience that changed his life. "I chose to put an end, deliberately, to hatred. . . . I chose for love. Terrorism is hatred and you can't live on hatred."

Mercier returned to Canada. The following year he travelled around the Gaspé Peninsula to try to raise money to help "political prisoners" still in Quebec jails. He wanted to use the money to buy them books and magazines. As an ex-terrorist he felt he might be able to draw some attention to the fund-raising effort. He stopped in small towns and spoke with the local radio and newspaper reporters. In all, he got about twenty-five dollars in donations. It barely paid for the gasoline.

Mercier forgot about politics. But the police had long memories. During the October Crisis he was made to pay for his crimes a second time. He and his wife were interned under the detention provisions of the War Measures Act. Mercier was held without charge for twelve days. His wife was held eight days.

In 1971 G-section was sifting through old reports, looking for likely informers. Mercier's file had been inactive for some time, but it appeared that he might have maintained his contacts with suspected terrorists. He certainly had the credentials to infiltrate into a suspected group. They decided it was time to have a talk with Louis Mercier again.

Mercier worked nights as a grocery warehouseman to support his artistic endeavours. He was heading home from work on the morning of October 20, stopping first at his mother's house in Rosemount to use the shower because his small apartment didn't have one. He left his mother's and drove towards his home along Holt Street. A car was parked against the curb. Mercier started to pull around it when another car pulled alongside his. The passenger signalled for him to pull over. Mercier got out to see what was up. The men who had stopped him were Cpls. Bernard Dubuc and Normand Chamberland. One said, "Just a minute, Mercier. I want to talk with you." Mercier agreed, "Sure. Come to my place." That wasn't what the men had in mind. Mercier had no doubt that these were policemen. He also realized that he wasn't under arrest. But he was curious enough to go along with them. When he got into the unmarked car he thought he was going to a police station. Instead, Dubuc and Chamberland drove Mercier to a restaurant on Pie IX Boulevard. The three went inside for coffee. There was some small talk. The Mounties explained that they wanted to take Mercier to a nearby motel room where they could talk quietly. They couldn't take him to RCMP offices because the offices might be watched. Someone, perhaps a terrorist suspect, would see Mercier and Mercier would be compromised. His effectiveness as an informer would be destroyed.

Mercier agreed to go to the motel. In the room the policemen told him that they would pay for information about terrorist groups. Mercier said that he wasn't interested. Those days were behind him and he didn't want to get mixed up with those kinds of people again. The conversation was pleasant enough and lasted for more than an hour. But in the back of Mercier's mind he felt the police could cause him trouble—perhaps by planting drugs on him or taking him out to the woods for some rough stuff. It would be his word against theirs. "I have a criminal record. They don't," he said. His wife was waiting and he was anxious to get home. He stalled Dubuc and Chamberland, telling them that he would think about it and would meet them again in a few days at a pre-arranged room at the Laurentian Hotel.

On the day of the meeting Mercier told his wife that if she hadn't heard from him by a certain time she was to phone his lawyer and tell him about the appointment at the Laurentian Hotel. Mercier met Dubuc and Chamberland on time. He got right to the point. He wasn't interested, but if he heard anything about plans for violent action he would phone them. He didn't want any money, however. That would be an insult. He left without incident. The men of G-section were no further ahead in their attempts to recruit informants and Mercier wondered if his record would haunt him all the rest of his life.

A week later Mercier was fired from his job in the warehouse. Two years later a Mountie showed up at his apartment when he was away. The Mountie told Mrs. Mercier that he was investigating her husband for UIC fraud. As he poked around the apartment he told her that her husband's painting looked like communist art. They were paintings of nudes and landscapes. The Mountie left and nothing more was heard. Mercier testified at the McDonald Commission hearings in 1978. Although his testimony was generally favourable for the RCMP, the force's lawyer trotted out the criminal record to try to discredit Mercier's evidence and to show that Mercier was a "terrorist and a damned liar." RCMP lawyer Pierre Lamontagne's cross-examination was brutal. He even wanted Mercier to admit to a shoplifting charge that had nothing to do with Mercier's student-radical days. When Lamontagne was finished Mercier had the last word. "I was charged with crimes. I was a terrorist. . . . I paid for my crimes. I've been harassed. In the October Crisis they put me in jail. I want to live peacefully. . . . I'm paying for crimes I've already paid for. I'm being put on trial. Why? If you hated me so much before, do you have to hate me forever?"

Lionel Vachon's only scrape with the law came when he was nineteen and he broke a garage window. He had been drinking. A taxi driver saw him and called the police. In court Vachon explained that he was drunk and the charge was dismissed. That broken window was about the most exciting thing in Vachon's life until one night in November 1971 when two Mounties scooped him off the street and took him to a motel for an all-night interrogation.

Vachon was a childhood friend of Michel Lavoie, Marc Bouchard's friend. Vachon, a timid and shy twenty-year-old, kept up the acquaintance. He did odd jobs in his spare time and he was doing some house renovations for Lavoie. Vachon's regular job was as a clerk in Eaton's toy department. Vachon left work on the evening of November 10 and caught a bus for home. His stop was about a block from his house. He got off and started to cross a small park as a shortcut. As he neared his front door he noticed a man standing in the shadows on the street. It was Sergeant Hugo. Hugo identified himself as a policeman. He frisked Vachon and asked the young man to get into the unmarked car parked at the curb. Cpl. Paul Langlois was the driver. Vachon got into the backseat of the two-door car. Hugo rode in the front next to Langlois.

The policemen didn't say what they wanted. They drove to a restaurant and took Vachon inside with them. They ordered sandwiches. Vachon was nervous and upset and he couldn't eat. The policemen told Vachon that they just wanted to get to know him better. Vachon figured he'd better say something so he started to talk about the two-year hitch he spent in the navy. He went into elaborate detail about what it was like to work in a ship's boiler room. "I'm nervous by nature.... They said they just wanted to get to know me better and know what I was doing," Vachon told the McDonald Commission. When Langlois and Hugo finished their food they took Vachon out to the car again. There they started to ask about his friendship with Lavoie. They left the city and headed along Highway 25 until they came to a motel. Langlois registered for the room. Inside Vachon had fits of nervousness. The policemen recognized that he was frightened. Vachon was so scared that it never occurred to him to ask if he was free to leave even when Langlois told him specifically he wasn't under arrest. "When you are trying to develop a source you don't use a club," Langlois testified. The night was pretty much a repeat of the night spent with Doucet. The Mounties began to realize that Vachon was totally apolitical and that his little world revolved around his job in the toy department. They had pegged him for an FLQ sympathizer because of his relationship with Lavoie, but they were wrong. He couldn't be of any use to the police. At about 8:15 a.m.—more than thirteen hours after they had picked him up—Langlois and Hugo drove Vachon back into town and dropped him off at a Metro station. Vachon went straight to work. In an official report the Mounties described Vachon as "timid with limited intelligence."

When Bouchard and Lavoie decided that they should drop from sight they needed a place to stay outside the city. They had a friend, a stage-lighting technician, who helped them out by introducing them to Robert Racine. Bouchard and Lavoie were introduced under assumed names. Racine was a lighting-equipment salesman who owned a farm in the country. He was pleased to let the two new acquaintances stay at his farm if they helped out with chores and tended things. Racine's generosity to strangers got him into trouble with the Security Service and cost him his job.

Racine and his wife lived in a high-rise apartment on Île des Soeurs in Montreal. They went to the farm in the Eastern Townships only on weekends and had no way of knowing what Bouchard and Lavoie were up to during the week. But the Security Service thought that they did. A surveillance team carefully observed the men. The Mounties knew that they had a small-calibre rifle with them. From wiretaps they learned that Bouchard and Lavoie were talking about moving some "material" to the farm. With no other evidence, the Security Service concluded this might be dynamite.

G-section investigators Serge Boisvert and Louis Duhamel were assigned to the case. A plan was devised to raid the farmhouse and search for dynamite and any documents that might implicate Bouchard and Lavoie in terrorist activity. But before the raid the investigators wanted a chance to see if they could get the farm owner, Racine, to act as an informant. He might be more valuable in the long run than anything the police might find on the farm. On the evening of January 17, 1972, the raiding party

stood by about two miles from the farm while Duhamel and Boisvert made a call on Racine. The Mounties arrived at the apartment and identified themselves. They beat around the bush for a
few minutes and asked about the farm. Racine found it irksome
that the police would seem to know so much about his property.
The Mounties finally asked what Racine knew about his farm
tenants, Bouchard and Lavoie. Racine said he didn't know the
men by those names. When the Mounties told him Bouchard and
Lavoie were suspected terrorists, Racine was shocked. He felt that
he was caught up in something he knew nothing about—caught
between some people who he thought might be a little bit subversive and the police who were now asking him to serve as an informer. Racine said he didn't want any part of it. "I was the
cheese in the sandwich," he said. The police made some sugges-
tions that led him to think they suspected him of being in on it all
as part of the FLQ. Before they left the Mounties took a look
around the apartment and complimented Racine on his taste.
There was no mention of the impending search at the farm.

When they got outside Duhamel and Boisvert radioed for the
raiding party to begin the search. Five Mounties and members of
the Quebec Police Force moved in. The QPF was there ostensibly
because it had authority under the Quebec Explosives Act to
search for dynamite. But the RCMP was calling the shots. There
was no regular search warrant and the raid may have been illegal.
The raiders found no dynamite, no illegal contraband, no plans
for terrorist activity. They found nothing out of the ordinary.
They made no arrests. They had no evidence that their suspicions
about Bouchard and Lavoie were based on anything but rumour.

When Racine learned that his farm had been searched without
a warrant he was angry. He contacted the provincial ombudsman
and a prominent Montreal civil liberties lawyer to see what he
could do. Racine talked about writing a letter of complaint to the
RCMP. The Mounties knew all about it before the letter was written. They had learned about it from a wiretap. Racine was sound-
ing like he might cause some trouble.

Staff Sgt. Marc Leduc had an idea. He told Dubuc that he
should call on Racine's employer and plant some hints about his
association with terrorists in an attempt to get him fired. Dubuc

wasn't familiar with the case. If Leduc told him it was true, then Racine must be mixed up with the FLQ. Dubuc followed orders.

Dubuc visited the lighting company's personnel manager. The manager was asked about Racine's employment record. Racine had been with the company for four years. He won a top sales-man's award each year. Dubuc did some improvising and told the manager that his top salesman was using a company car to drive terrorists around the countryside. Dubuc did his job well. Racine was fired, the company said, for misuse of expenses relating to the company car. The excuse was so obviously phoney that Ra-cine thought there must be another reason. Maybe the company was upset because he had taken a lot of sick leave. It was only years later that he learned from a former colleague that the Mounties had been in to see the personnel manager.

The loss of the job was a severe financial blow. Racine and his wife sold the farm. He could get only short-term jobs and he was out of work for about half the year. Racine eventually made a financial recovery. He bought another farm and the ugly en-counter with the Mounties was in the past. But just before the 1976 Olympics three policemen showed up at the farm. Racine was out in the field when they arrived. Mrs. Racine was so star-tled she didn't take notice what force they were from. The men searched the farmhouse. They didn't show a warrant. And they left.

Cpl. Bernard Blier was new to G-section in Montreal in Septem-ber 1971. He had just been transferred from the two-member Se-curity Service detail at the Trois Rivières detachment. He didn't have any contacts in the separatist underground and getting con-tacts was a top priority. But he thought of someone in Trois Rivières who might be a suitable candidate. The man was Yvon Roy, a gregarious and friendly petty crook and con artist. Roy was serving his probation in Trois Rivières.

Roy never much minded being the centre of attention. During the October Crisis he was in Europe and he passed himself off as an expert on Quebec separatist politics for a Swiss TV show. He was back in Trois Rivières the following year and had his first official contact with Blier. Roy was wanted by Montreal police for petty fraud and Blier picked him up. Roy was soon released and was back in Trois Rivières to serve his probation. Police and petty criminals in a small town often find themselves in each other's company. They tend to have an understanding of what the other person is all about. Roy became friendly with RCMP Cpl. Pierre Bédard, Blier's old partner. Bédard visited Roy in the motel room where Roy was living. He dropped in to see what Roy was up to and the two men watched the end of a hockey game together. Then Roy was taken to the police station where he was asked insulting questions about how he dressed and how he combed his hair.

Roy served his probation as the supervisor of about twenty other probationers working on a Local Initiatives Program project to build a community recreation centre for Trois Rivières. It was the kind of project where the local politicians showed up to have their pictures taken for the newspaper.

Roy was also a member of the local citizens' committee, which was involved with the recreation centre project. The group organized a softball league for teenage girls and printed a small community newspaper. It was the sort of group, Roy says, where "half the people were more or less handicapped. There was no subversive activity. Oh, they would vote against the party in power." The police, however, were suspicious of this form of Trois Rivières civic activism. There were, for example, pot smokers in the group. A cat and mouse game developed. The pot smokers would hide their stash whenever they saw one of the policemen at a softball game or along the street. They would make jokes about the men from the RCMP being from the Gestapo. The fun was in pretending that one side was up to more than the other side knew about.

Blier found himself in another world in Montreal. His transfer brought him new stature with his former colleagues in Trois Rivières. In the early spring of 1972 Blier returned to his old detachment with a special mission. He was going to try to recruit his old nemesis, Roy, and turn him into an informer. Bédard and the other Mounties at Trois Rivières were impressed by this "specialist coming from Montreal with new methods." Blier's new method was to try to scare Roy into cooperating by making him believe that there were arrest warrants out for him.

The men at the local detachment phoned Roy and asked him to come to the detachment office. Roy was upset, because "the police don't usually give you boxes of chocolates or flowers." He didn't know what it was about. He called his lawyer in Montreal who didn't have a clue either. This was unusual. When the police wanted to talk to Roy they usually picked him up. This time he had to take a cab to their office. "I respect the police. They phoned...I went," he told the McDonald Commission. When he arrived he was ushered into the small Security Service office where Blier was waiting.

Roy recalls that Blier began the conversation by saying, "I've got bad news for you. I've got warrants for you." Blier opened his suit jacket and showed Roy some legal forms in the inside pocket. From time to time Blier would flash the papers to impress Roy with the serious problems the man might be facing if he didn't cooperate. It was a charade. The forms were blank. Roy wasn't wanted for anything. Yet he was made to believe for a time that the sword of Damocles hung over his head.

The men fenced for awhile. Blier wanted Roy to spy on the citizens' committee. Roy demanded to know what the warrants were for. When Blier wouldn't tell him, Roy suspected a bluff. He felt the warrants were intended as some kind of blackmail, but Blier wasn't a very convincing actor. When the ruse didn't work Blier left. Bédard drove Roy home. The Mountie told Roy to have a couple of cognacs and to forget the whole thing. "Once you have a record you're always somewhat afraid," Roy testified.

Roy's criminal record came up again during McDonald Commission hearings. Lamontagne, the RCMP lawyer, tried to impeach Roy's credibility even though his story was substantially the same as Blier's. Roy challenged Lamontagne to step outside in the hallway where they could settle the matter man-to-man.

Raymond Tremblay was a law student working for a storefront legal clinic when he had his encounter with the Security Service. The clinic, known as Commune Juridique, was on St. Denis Street.

Some of the lawyers defended FLQ members. The Security Service, wanting to know what the lawyers were up to, planned to bug the lawyer-prisoner interview room in one of the jails. Headquarters killed the idea because it would cause a flap if it were ever discovered.

Undaunted, G-section thought it could get information from an informer and Tremblay seemed to be a likely candidate. Tremblay, twenty-seven, was in debt and could use money. He owed $4,000 and the bank was threatening to take his car. Blier was assigned to the case.

Blier started by trying to tail Tremblay around town. He wasn't very successful. An experienced surveillance team was assigned to help out. On the morning of June 7, 1972, Tremblay left his house and started to drive towards the courthouse. The surveillance team notified Blier at RCMP offices. Blier and his driver, Const. Richard Daigle, headed out to make the interception. At the intersection of Amhurst and Ontario Streets an unmarked RCMP car stopped dead in front of Tremblay's car. The student tried to back up, but a second unmarked car blocked the rear. A third car, driven by Daigle, swung into the intersection and Blier jumped out. He reached for his badge and in the excitement dropped it on the pavement. He picked it up and quickly flashed it at Tremblay. He didn't want the student to get a good look because he didn't want it known that the men were from the RCMP. The badge, however, would have the desired psychological effect. Tremblay remembers Blier calling him by name and saying, "Tremblay, come with us. We're picking you up. We're going to the police station." Blier remembers it slightly differently. The flashing of the badge was to reassure the student that he wasn't being kidnapped. He says he told the student that he wasn't under arrest, but that the police knew he had financial problems and they could help. "He was somewhat surprised," Blier recalls. But if Tremblay was really worried and thought he was being kidnapped by imposters posing as policemen "he could have yelled for help for the police," Blier told the McDonald Commission. "But you were the police," Commissioner Guy Gilbert reminded him.

Tremblay offered no resistance. From his legal training he

knew that he could be charged with resisting arrest. He thought the police were arresting him for drug possession. Tremblay got into the backseat of the four-door car. Blier sat next to him and Daigle drove. The Mounties say Tremblay could have left at any time. But his choices were to jump out of a moving car or stay.

Tremblay was frightened. He kept denying that he was involved in drugs or anything else that might be illegal. Blier wanted him to quit talking about drugs. Besides, "I couldn't tell the difference between coke and marijuana," Blier told the McDonald Commission. Tremblay thought he was going to a police station until Daigle headed across the Jacques Cartier Bridge and out of town. Tremblay then began to wonder if this might be the anti-terrorist squad of the Montreal police. Blier told him that they were going to a spot across the U.S. border for a week. Daigle drove along Highway 3 and then turned on to Highway 20, the Trans-Canada Highway towards Quebec City. Tremblay wanted it to end and he turned around, trying to attract the attention of someone in another car. Blier tapped him on the head and told him to keep his eyes in front of him. "It was like theatre," Tremblay recalls.

As the car sped along Blier started to explain that they wanted Tremblay to become a paid informer. The money could be deposited quietly in Tremblay's bank account and nobody would be the wiser. Tremblay felt that the offer had an aspect of a threat to it.

About twenty miles outside the city, near Ste-Madeleine, Daigle pulled the car off the main highway and on to a secondary road. He found a deserted dirt path surrounded by bushes. He drove along the path for several hundred yards. The interrogation continued for more than an hour. At one point Blier asked to see Tremblay's wallet. Tremblay remembers that when he wouldn't provide the wallet Blier moved to take it from the student's pocket. At that moment Tremblay thought he had Blier off balance and he gave Blier a shove and tried to get out of the car. When he reached for the door handle it wouldn't open. Blier grabbed him. Daigle turned around in the front seat to help Blier. The policemen pushed Tremblay's head down and Blier held him in an arm lock. Tremblay gave up any thought of escaping.

Daigle and Blier tell the story differently. Blier says it was

Tremblay who started it by trying to jump at him and shove him. Blier reached across and locked the car door. His motives were compassionate. He felt Tremblay was demoralized and he didn't want to leave him alone in the middle of nowhere. Blier acknowledges that he held Tremblay in an arm lock for maybe ten minutes. Daigle agrees with this version and says that possibly he helped Blier to calm Tremblay by holding one of the student's arms.

Tremblay gave up. But he couldn't help the police even if he had wanted to. He didn't know anything about the FLQ criminal cases. His work involved civil cases. Tremblay soon got bored with all this and he began to ignore the questioning. He listened to the birds. It went on for awhile longer and then Tremblay was told he was free. But, according to Tremblay, Blier gave him a warning: "You better watch your step. We can come back. You might find yourself by the roadside and you might be digging your own grave." Neither Daigle nor Blier recall any such threat.

The policemen say they offered to drive Tremblay back to Montreal, but the student turned them down because he had friends living nearby who could give him a lift. Tremblay says he was told to wait on the path for five minutes and then he would be free to leave. He was abandoned there and the policemen drove off. Tremblay never learned until much later that the men were from the RCMP.

Tremblay walked along the path and stopped for a little while at a hut in the woods. He then continued on towards the main highway for about fifteen minutes until he found a house. The owner let him use the phone to call the law commune. One of the lawyers came and picked him up. When he got back to town Tremblay found his car had been parked on Amhurst Street in a no parking zone. There was a ticket on it.

The next day Blier wrote a misleading report about the incident. It suggested that Tremblay had agreed to become an informer. It made no mention of the interlude in the woods.

Tremblay told one of the senior lawyers in the commune what had happened. The lawyer had a friend who had been the victim of a similar incident. The following week the lawyer held a press conference and called for Quebec Justice Minister Jérôme Choquette to investigate the incidents. Short stories appeared in *Le Devoir* and the *Gazette*. But nothing more happened.

Blier, however, had to update his report to explain the incident in the woods. He wrote that Tremblay embellished and twisted the story of the "acquaintance interview" to enhance his stature with the commune. The student tricked the Mounties into thinking he would become an informer. Blier looked for the silver lining. He wrote that he and Daigle had been wise not to trust Tremblay with the knowledge of what force they were with.

Some of G-section's attempts to recruit informers were described in graphic detail in a report forwarded to headquarters. The report was written by Marie-Claire Dubé, G-section's young analyst, who, Cobb said, impressed people in the section even though they had a tendency "to have funny thoughts about people who are [university] educated." Her report said that when Vachon, the toy department clerk, was intercepted he was frightened and he expected that he would be hit by Sergeant Hugo. The entire incident "tended to terrorize our subject," she wrote. The report said Blier visited Roy in Trois Rivières "to threaten [him] with two false arrest warrants." It mentioned that Doucet was treated like a child and was made to stand in a corner. Doucet "went through a series of trances." The report said that "it was hardly surprising" that Racine lost his job after the Mounties talked with his personnel manager.

Rational and reasonable people reading the report might have asked themselves what was going on in G-section. There might have been some demand for a further explanation or an order to stop the rough stuff. Instead, the report was sent along to headquarters with a forwarding note by Cobb that "the efforts put in by all are commendable and very much encouraged here." (Cobb later claimed that he hadn't read the entire report before it was forwarded.) Peter Marwitz, an analyst at headquarters, got the report, read it and sent it to superiors with a note saying that "it looks like a good, though likely temporary, disruption tactic by Montreal." Nobody at headquarters thought there was anything wrong with these G-section activities.

It was only when the McDonald Commission was about to release the report that the RCMP tried to discredit it as the work of a young, naive woman with an overactive imagination. The evidence of the victims indicates just the opposite—that indeed G-section employed strong-arm tactics to try to intimidate potential informers. If anything, the Dubé report was understated. What happened to some of the victims sounded startlingly like the legal description of kidnapping.

Cobb testified that not all of G-section's recruiting attempts were failures. He argued that even the seven cases heard by the McDonald Commission represented some successes of sorts. The plans of suspected terrorists were disrupted when they learned that the Security Service was on to them. The recruitment attempts fit rather nicely into the pattern established with the 1971 policy documents on disruptive tactics, the infamous "disruption— coercion and compromise" policy drafted by headquarters.

The McDonald Commission uncovered a disturbing footnote to these events. The Dubé report was originally prepared as a discussion document to be used in training seminars for other units because headquarters thought G-section was doing good work.

5

The PQ Tapes

The plan to steal the membership lists of the Parti Québécois started with one small kernel of information obtained by a low-ranking member of the Security Service. By the time that the plan was executed, it had involved the highest-ranking officers, including Director-General John Starnes. It began in the summer of 1972, when Cpl. Maurice Goguen of Montreal's G-section spotted a magazine article describing how the PQ had grown to the point where it kept its membership records on computer storage tapes. G-section was compiling a mountain of information about the separatist party. There was the worry that terrorists might be following Pierre Vallières' suggestion to join the PQ. The Security Service wanted to know who was signing up.

Goguen also obtained a copy of the PQ membership application card. The card had blanks for name, address, marital status, date of birth, occupation, employer, phone number, riding and amount of political contribution. That kind of data would be invaluable to the Security Service. Goguen gathered together other bits and pieces of information. On August 8 he sat down and prepared a detailed memorandum for his superiors in Montreal.

The memorandum reported that the PQ shared a Burroughs B500 computer with Les Editions Peladeau, a Montreal newspaper printing enterprise. The computer was located at the offices of the newspaper distributing firm, Les Messageries Dynamiques, at 9820 Jeanne-Mance Street in an industrial area at the north end of Montreal. The clipping from the magazine included a photograph of a computer operator working at a 3M terminal at PQ headquarters at 5675 Christophe-Colomb Avenue. Goguen also reported that Edouard Cloutier, a professor at the Montreal campus of the University of Quebec, was responsible for compiling some kind of statistics for the PQ.

Goguen recommended that R.E. Meyer, the officer in charge of the software and operations branch for the RCMP's giant Canadian Police Information Centre (CPIC) computer, be asked "the ways and possibilities of gaining access to the information that the Parti Québécois has on computer." Meyer was a former Burroughs employee and Goguen thought he might still have a trustworthy company contact who could help out.

Three days later the special services section of the Security Service in Montreal sent a top secret Telex message to Ottawa headquarters outlining Goguen's proposal. Even at this early stage of planning the operation was assigned a puma file number. Puma operations involved the clandestine copying of material, usually the photographing of documents after a surreptitious break-in. At this point, however, an actual break-in wasn't contemplated. Montreal only wanted to know if Ottawa's computer experts could think of "any possibility of gaining access to the information being registered in a computer and if so the procedures to follow to obtain the information without having to involve too many people." G-section in Montreal felt "the value of such an operation is great" and would provide updated information on separatist file subjects "as well as statistics on the degree of separatist infiltration of our key sectors—education, police and armed forces, and provincial and federal governments."

Officials in the Privy Council Office were also passing along rumours to the Security Service that the PQ was receiving substantial sums of money from foreign countries, particularly France. The Ottawa government was suspicious of the meddlesome French ever since General Charles de Gaulle's "*Vive Québec libre*" speech on the steps of Montreal's city hall in 1967. The computer tapes might provide PQ financing information that could confirm whether there was any basis for these rumours.

Staff Sgt. Ken Hollas at headquarters technical services branch passed the problem along to one of his subordinates, Sgt. H.E. Reed, with a note saying that "when you have formulated a plan of action discuss with me please." Ten days later headquarters Telexed Montreal with discouraging news. The computer experts in Ottawa felt "that it is most unlikely that the PQ would not take sufficient security precautions to prevent a terminal and phone extraction of information." It didn't seem technically possible to tap into the computer bank from outside. The possibility of a tap wasn't abandoned entirely. Headquarters wanted Montreal to find out if the PQ system was an on-line system and whether another computer user shared the system if it was on-line. But Burroughs officials couldn't provide much help even if it was an on-line system. However, the experts said, "the best means of obtaining the desired info is through one of the computer analysts at the scene [with] access to the tapes or cards." The Montreal unit might also try recruiting one of the keypunch operators at Les Messageries Dynamiques.

By September the code name Ham was being used in the planning documents. Also that month Hollas sent the Montreal unit an article about data security from *Canadian Datasystems* magazine. The article was spotted by Ken Burnett, a CPIC computer expert and civilian member of the force who had been recruited by Hollas and Reed to consider the technical problems in circumventing computer security protections. The article was disheartening for the men in Montreal. It described a number of safeguards, such as passwords, to protect computer data. However, there was one glimmer of hope. The article stated: "It is self-evident, but absolutely true, that there is no way of guaranteeing total security, of guaranteeing that someone who wants access to confidential data cannot with sufficient time and money do so." The RCMP had both the time and the money—and the determination.

In mid-October, Montreal sent an updating report to headquarters indicating that limited progress had been made. It was determined that no outside terminals fed the computer on Jeanne-Mance Street. "Anyone wishing to use the computer must go to the above address." There was no luck in trying to recruit a friendly employee or keypunch operator. "Developing a source within this company is considered too risky in view of the nature of this investigation and the possible political issues that could materialize. However, we have not eliminated the idea completely and may consider it later."

A former member of the force, Jim Emberg, who was working as a sales representative for a business-forms systems company, was cautiously approached for assistance. He proved to be an important figure in the operation. Emberg, who also had experience as a Bell Telephone employee, kept his contacts with his former colleagues in the RCMP. On occasion he "volunteered his experience" for Criminal Investigations Branch (CIB) operations.

After several conversations with Emberg, "it was decided that we would have to place him in our confidence if we had any further intentions of furthering this investigation," the October report said. Emberg learned that Les Messageries Dynamiques had twelve to twenty hours of computer time available for outside work during weekends at a rate of $200 an hour. Emberg's company had the contract for business forms for Les Messageries Dynamiques and he could arrange a visit to the location without arousing suspicion. "We also discovered that the information is stored on disks and that there is no security coding to draw the information." (Many of the subsequent RCMP documents concerning Operation Ham mistakenly refer to computer "disks" rather than tapes.) Emberg believed the majority of the employees at Les Messageries Dynamiques were Parti Québécois sympathizers. This seemed to reduce any hope of trying to recruit a friendly source within the company.

Some preliminary surveillance work showed that there was a lot of traffic near the area during the week, but on weekends things were pretty quiet. "There appear to be extensive patrols at night and during weekends by Montreal police and other private security agencies. The target has an alarm system . . . ," the report continued.

Meanwhile, there was a meeting involving Staff Sgt. G. Albert and Corporals Goguen and Dale Boire from Montreal G-section, and Ken Burnett and Insp. C. Yule, the CPIC computer people from Ottawa. Yule and Burnett explained what additional information was needed to determine how to deal with the computer security problems. On October 18, Emberg paid a visit to Dollard Desroches, the data-processing manager at Les Messageries Dynamiques. Emberg brought Burnett along. Burnett used an alias, Ken Burns, and arranged a cover story to explain his presence. The cover story even involved preparations to phone a friendly trucking company manager to confirm Burnett's identity as "Burns" as a backup if Desroches or anyone else got suspicious. The cover story wasn't needed and after a successful hourlong visit Emberg and Burnett left, convinced that Desroches was unaware that the men were casing the premises.

Montreal reported the results of the visit to Ottawa headquarters. "Our area of interest was outlined on a rough sketch. The exact location of our objective is on the second floor and in the rear. There was no visible interior security. The information we are after is stored on tapes in cabinets. There is a card index system in Desroches' office to let you know which tape to draw from the cabinet. The detailed technical aspect of the system may be best explained to you by Mr. Burnett. Please thank him for his assistance thus far."

In addition to the interior sketch, photographs were taken of the front and rear entrances of the building. There seemed little doubt that Operation Ham was moving towards a clandestine break-in job similar to G-section's earlier raid at L'Agence-Presse Libre du Québec.

The Montreal unit realized they were about to become involved in activities that required the strictest of security measures. Despite his previous service for the force, Emberg was given a new security form to sign. The form, known as an "indoctrination undertaking," advises the signer that he is participating in intelligence operations and that disclosure by him of what he knows would be "prejudicial to the safety and interest of Canada" and would leave him liable to prosecution under the Official Secrets Act.

Cpl. Gerard Boucher, a member of the security equipment section, a unit whose duties include a lot of lock pickings, was assigned to the Ham team. On October 19 he cased the Jeanne-Mance Street location from the outside. He inspected the alarm system, but couldn't determine whether it was hooked up to the offices of a burglary alarm or guard agency or whether it was attached to an alarm bell in the building. A peek through an open garage door determined that there was no alarm attached to that door. There were spotlights around the building at night. There was also an exterior fire escape running to the roof.

Montreal reported to Ottawa that "the alarm has an Ace lock and there is also a Viro lock on the door. Corporal Boucher will look into the possibility of obtaining more information through one of his contacts."

The October 19 report summarized the current state of the planning: "Our present standing is to: (a) Establish a contact that will be able to copy a tape to another tape on a short notice and most likely on a Sunday (the target is empty every Sunday except for one Sunday a month). This contact will be recruited in such a way that he will not know that the force is involved. (b) Establish a secure method of entry that can be employed on other future dates. This means that we would conduct a couple of dry runs in order to determine the exact place of entry, the interior route to our objective as well as the time required for such an operation." The job was tentatively scheduled for late November or early December.

On November 7 Ottawa asked for a further update. Specifically, could Emberg establish a contact in Montreal who could copy a seven-track tape to a nine-track? Burnett in Ottawa knew a local company with a branch in Montreal that might be able to do the job. Burnett could also provide a seven-track tape for a dry run. He felt that the time factor was important, that it might take up to thirty minutes to locate the correct PQ tape and that copying time would take up to an hour. The next day Montreal Telexed back that Emberg knew that the local IBM office was open twenty-four hours a day. But IBM would require seven-days notice for copying work and charged $700 an hour. Montreal also wanted to know if the unit could borrow Corporal Boucher again for a couple of dry run break-ins.

The planning was well advanced. But in mid-November everything that had been done by the Security Service men seemed legal. Dry run break-ins were a second, far more serious and risky phase of Operation Ham. Approval had to be obtained by some senior authority before events proceeded any further.

On November 14 Insp. J.A. Nowlan, Ken Hollas' boss in Ottawa's technical services branch, went to Chief Supt. Howard Draper, one of Starnes' deputies, to get the go-ahead. The approval document outlined the plan to get PQ membership lists as a result of an entry. It said that G-section was interested in the Parti Québécois only in so far as it might be used "as a vehicle by revolutionaries or agents of foreign power. Since the Vallières declaration of one year ago the revolutionary movement has turned in the direction of the PQ and there is now good evidence of a strong radical-left waffle group within the party. Of concern also is the incursions made by péquistes [PQ members] into all levels of government. A recent survey done by G Operations revealed that there are 235 péquistes holding positions within federal government departments. Our information in this area is so limited that the survey is considered to be less than 50 per cent accurate and that the actual figure must be much higher.

"By necessity our investigational techniques have been curtailed because of the political ramifications. It is hoped that the information which might be gained from the operation would provide sufficient data to properly assess the degree of revolutionary influence within the party and the impact the PQ can exert through its influence in government departments. It is requested that this operation be approved in principle." Draper signed it with the note: "Approved in principle. No action beyond study at this time."

That afternoon Montreal was notified of Draper's action, but was warned that "in view of the possible political ramifications it is emphasized that further investigation is not to go beyond that which is necessary to determine problems, possible risks, etc. ...."

Corporal Boucher, the lock man, was sent back to Montreal two days later to help with planning. From 11:30 p.m. to 1 a.m. on the night of November 16-17 Boucher and Ward Jones, a civilian member in the same security equipment section, conducted an exterior survey of the building. A Sergeant Gard acted as a lookout at the front entrance and Goguen covered the rear. Boucher and

Jones, according to a later report, felt confident they could enter the building through the garage door in short order. "They will develop some equipment they would like to use," the report said. "The target has trucks remaining in their yard overnight. Last night there was one right in front of the target on the street. Security equipment has an almost identical vehicle minus the markings. Boucher has offered the use of their truck to be used near the target for coverage purposes. We agree with this idea and will arrange to have Quebec license plates available." The plan was to use the truck to drive the Mounties right up to the door. The report from Montreal also complained about the radio equipment that was to be used. "We have used these radios on numerous operations and we have experienced some sort of communication problem constantly.... We are required to repeat our transmissions several times to make contact. Last night the radios were tested in our office before the survey. In the target area we were unable to communicate a distance of approximately two hundred feet.... In operations such as this one we cannot afford to rely on radios which are not dependable."

On November 20 Montreal advised headquarters that a likely computer firm, MICR Systems Limited, had been found at Westmount Square, about a twenty- or thirty-minute drive from Jeanne-Mance Street. MICR had an optical scanner which could copy seven-track to nine-track. The only contact with MICR was through Emberg, who didn't reveal that the copying work was for the RCMP. The next day Montreal also reported that the print shop in the target building printed Parti Québécois literature. This just about killed any thought of the Mounties trying to recruit a source within the building.

A week after his approval in principle, Draper signed a further authorization for Ham. This one authorized another physical survey "which may require entry." The approval form, like the first one of November 14, was prepared and signed by Nowlan. It said that planning had progressed to the point where there was one remaining problem—securing safe entry. At least one more survey would be required. The following day Ottawa headquarters Telexed Draper's response. "Authority to proceed with a further survey as outlined ... has been approved." However, Ottawa wanted to know what progress Montreal was making with the alarm system problem.

For Staff Sergeant Albert and Corporal Boire of Montreal's special services branch, Christmas came early. On November 21 they interviewed the owner of the company that had installed the alarm system and "he was very cooperative and answered all our questions without hesitation," a report the next day said. Albert and Boire gradually swung their conversation of alarm systems around to the one at 9820 Jeanne-Mance Street. The Mounties told the alarm systems man that they were investigating a pornography ring that was suspected of printing its material at the shop in the building. The man, whose name was deleted from documents made public by the McDonald Commission to protect his privacy, said that the alarm at the target building hadn't been serviced in eighteen months. He provided the key number for the Ace lock for the alarm system on the front door. He told the Mounties that when the system was installed some doors on the second floor were also wired to the alarm. But he also told them that the control box for the system was beneath the stairs just inside the front door. The entire system could be turned off with the same front door alarm key. As an extra Christmas present, the man gave the Mounties some spare keys he had lying about to see if any of them would work. One of them did.

At about midnight on November 23, Albert, Boire, Sergeant Gard, a Cpl. Y. Beaulieu, civilian member Jones and Corporal Boucher, the lock men, staked out the building. But there were people inside. The team came back at 3 a.m. and found the building was still occupied. The dry run was postponed for a week.

Burnett, the CPIC computer man, was kept busy preparing his end of the operation in Ottawa. He made two dummy seven-track tapes to see how well the MICR equipment could copy to nine-track.

November 30 began with a Staff Sgt. N. Luker and a L. Bisson going with Boire to interview the alarm company owner a second time. Some more technical information was explained. That night the men in Montreal completed their first dry run break-in at the target. Corporal Beaulieu and a Constable Richer took up surveillance at the front of the building. Sergeant Gard and Corporal Goguen watched the rear. Corporal Boire watched the door. Boucher and Jones were assigned the task of actual entry. They were the technical experts, the professionals who knew how to open locks. The men cautiously approached the building at 11:30 p.m. and saw that the building was empty. They discovered that the front door alarm wasn't working. Their Ace lock key was tested and worked. The men banged on the windows to see if alarm bells would sound anywhere. They heard none. They then scampered back to their cars and waited to see if the Montreal police or private security guards would respond to an undetected silent alarm. Nothing happened. An hour later the men again took up their positions. Boucher and Jones entered. Boucher quickly located the alarm box and shut off the system. The two men headed upstairs where they ran into a problem, a Natcor lock. This was a new kind of lock for Boucher and Jones. The pair worked away inside for about forty-five minutes and then decided to call it a night. Outside, the lookouts saw that there was a constant flow of trucks to and from the building. But these seemed to be drivers dropping off newspaper receipts before heading home. The drivers didn't appear to notice anything suspicious.

Two days later, an early Sunday morning, a test to set the timing from Jeanne-Mance Street to the MICR office at Westmount Square was carried out. Sometime around 3 a.m. Ken Burnett left his home in Ottawa with the dummy computer tapes he had prepared. He drove to Montreal where he met the others at about 5:30 a.m. At 6 a.m. Albert, Boire and Burnett drove the dummy tapes to Victoria Hall in Westmount. There Burnett met up with Emberg and the two went on alone to the MICR offices. The dummy tapes were copied without a hitch. The return to Jeanne-Mance Street was just a reversal of the departure. The entire job took eighty-five minutes, but the Mounties felt they could have cut this if there hadn't been a snow storm. On this basis they figured the final operation, including an entry, would take no more than two hours.

With this, the men planned another dry run entry for the following Thursday and the actual operation the next Sunday. A detailed plan was drawn up and Telexed to Ottawa. The Montreal unit had determined that about thirty employees had access to the building. They contemplated keeping surveillance on the employees to make sure they were all quietly at home tucked into bed during the break-in. But the idea was rejected because it would tie up too much manpower. Spot checks at irregular hours showed that an early morning entry was probably the best time to avoid being discovered by an employee. The communications problem was solved with the borrowing of radios and walkie-talkies from other sections. Phone numbers at telephone booths at Victoria Hall and Westmount Square were noted and men were assigned to these points to receive any emergency messages that might have to be relayed while the tapes were in transit. A telephone-equipped observation post was planned for across the street. Car rentals were arranged so that no vehicle could be traced back to the RCMP. The assigned lookouts were instructed to detain anyone who might be headed for the building by asking for the time or a cigarette. The surveillance car operators could then radio those on the inside. This so-called "disaster plan" also required those entering the building not to carry identification of any kind. It was decided not to let Montreal municipal police know of the operation. This presented some risks. The building was in the area of Montreal Police Station 20. But the plan called for the observation-post men to notify a ranking senior officer, Insp. Claude Vermette, if those on the inside were caught. Vermette was then expected to contact Montreal police to "make the necessary arrangements." Backup vehicles were assigned to follow the cars from Jeanne-Mance Street to the Victoria Hall transfer point and then to Westmount Square. The planners didn't want any unforeseen traffic accident adding to the time it would take to return the original tapes. Radio transmitting equipment was to be left inside Les Messageries Dynamiques offices to detect if anyone entered somehow without being spotted by the lookouts.

That was the final plan. But the lock men wanted one more dry run to see if they had solved the Natcor lock problem. They tried on Thursday night, December 7, but they couldn't approach the building because it was occupied from 10 p.m. to 2:30 a.m. They gave up and went home. It was decided to conduct regular surveillance of the building from 6 p.m. to 7 a.m. for seven to ten days to see if a pattern of occupancy and vacancy could be determined. The owner of a building across the street was persuaded to allow the Mounties to set up their nocturnal observation post on his premises. A waiting game began.

It was only a matter of time now. Some of the brass in Ottawa began to show signs of nervousness. John Starnes, the director-general of the Security Service, was shown the final operational plan and he approved. Inspector Nowlan, the head of Ottawa's technical services branch, passed along a suggestion that not only should the PQ tapes be taken but several others as well. This would give the impression that "it was a case of industrial sabotage" if the Montreal men were caught in the midst of the operation or if some unforeseen foul-up prevented the return of the original tapes. (Montreal never followed up this suggestion.)

As an added security precaution, headquarters decided that while the duplicated computer tapes would be kept in Ottawa the information on them would be disseminated on a "need-to-know" basis only to G-section men in Montreal.

On December 12 Ken Burnett in Ottawa reported a snag in decoding the copies of the dummy tapes produced by MICR during the timing test. Emberg was dispatched to MICR to get additional technical information.

On December 13 Montreal reported the results of the surveillance work. It wasn't good news. Almost every night someone was working late inside the building. Additional help was obtained from I-section, the watcher service. I-section personnel do nothing except tail people. Many of the I-section staff are civilians, including women. The secret to their success is that they don't look like policemen and the tails are changed frequently so that the target doesn't become suspicious through seeing one individual near him for any considerable length of time.

Emberg got some of the additional information that Burnett had requested about the decoding problem. Burnett was told that if he needed further details he should phone a contact at OCR Concepts Limited, another Montreal computer firm. Burnett was reminded to use his alias, Ken Burns, and to call on a special direct line from Ottawa so that the OCR Concepts people wouldn't know he wasn't in Montreal.

The Montreal men reported continuing frustrations at the observation post. The final dry run entry, planned for December 14, was called off because the building was again occupied.

Three more nights of watching and waiting passed before the final dry run was completed. At 12:15 a.m. the observation post reported that the building was empty. Corporal Goguen took up his lookout station at the rear and Corporal Beaulieu and Constable Richer covered the front. Corporal Boire was at the door as Boucher and Jones, the lock experts, entered and went to work. While inside Boucher and Jones made a key for the second-floor office door. They copied the code number for a key to the filing cabinet where the tapes were stored. The manager's office, which had the index cards needed to identify the PQ tapes, was easily unlocked. The first card in the middle index drawer listed the PQ tapes as 00101. The card was right where Ken Burnett said it would be found. The two lock experts went around and unlocked all the other second-floor doors, including the computer room where the giant Burroughs machine whirred away unattended. With news of this success a final operation date was set for January 8. The Security Service men in Montreal and Ottawa enjoyed a Merry Christmas and looked forward to a successful New Year.

At 4:35 p.m. on January 8, 1973, the communications room at Security Service headquarters in Ottawa logged in a "Top Secret—Priority—Immediate Handling" Telex message from the special services unit in Montreal. It was hand delivered to Ken Hollas' desk in the technical services branch. It was short and to the point. "... arrangements have been made to conduct this operation tonight." The operational plan of December 5 was to be followed. There was one minor modification. The owner of the building across the street would no longer allow the Mounties to set up their observation point there. I-section, however, loaned them a vehicle as a mobile observation post. Hotel accommodations were confirmed for Burnett and Reed, the out-of-town computer experts.

At 11 p.m. a final briefing was held at the Security Service offices and then the men moved to take up their positions. Const. J.L. Boutin and Const. J. Delisle reported from the mobile observation post that the building was empty. The I-section watchers made sure that two employees who tended to work late at night were nowhere near the area on this occasion. Inspector Vermette and Staff Sgt. François d'Entremont waited together anxiously by the phone at the Security Service offices in case the disaster plan had to be implemented. Jim Emberg waited at Victoria Hall. Cpl. Y. Beaulieu and Const. M. Richer acted as lookouts at the front of 9820 Jeanne-Mance Street. Sgt. J. Gard and Cpl. Maurice Goguen, who started it all six months earlier with the first information about computerized PQ records, stood guard at the rear.

At 12:20 a.m. Boucher and Jones, the lock men, entered the building with their key. Staff Sgt. G. Albert and Cpl. Dale Boire moved in behind to provide inside security coverage. Boucher and Jones worked their way smoothly through the building, up the stairs, unlocking doors and moving on directly to the Parti Québécois tapes. The tapes were on their way to the Victoria Hall rendezvouz within minutes. From there Jim Emberg took them on the final leg to MICR at Westmount Square.

A problem. To the computer people at MICR it probably seemed only a minor problem that could be cleared up with a little time and patience. In the official report to headquarters it was described as a "few difficulties" in making the copies. The delay was never fully explained. But the clock ticked on. Two o'clock. Three o'clock. Four o'clock. Five o'clock. The Mounties waited. Finally, the copying job was complete. The original tapes were rushed back to Jeanne-Mance Street and the Mounties locked up the building at 5:15 a.m. Elapsed time, four hours and fifty-five minutes, almost three hours longer than originally planned.

After getting some sleep, Burnett and Reed returned to Ottawa to process the treasured copies of the tapes. In Ottawa and Montreal it was a time for summing up. Marie-Claire Dubé, the civilian analyst and unofficial historian for G-section in Montreal, was assigned to write a summary of the entire operation. She eventually produced a five-page chronological report that remains one of the most complete RCMP documents on Operation Ham. Lists were compiled of Security Service personnel who were directly or indirectly responsible for Ham's ultimate success. Early in the planning it was hoped that as few people as possible would be involved for security reasons. The lists, however, show that more than ninety people had some part in Operation Ham. Many, however, were the watchers from I-section who probably didn't have any idea why they were tailing people or even that the Parti Québécois was the target. Those who knew the full story probably never numbered more than a score.

The brass at G-section and the technical services branch at headquarters were delighted with the results. On January 11 they Telexed congratulations to Montreal "to express appreciation for the efforts put forth . . . in bringing this operation to a successful conclusion. We realize that many long hours were put in by all concerned in this most delicate operation." Draper also wired his personal congratulations.

Burnett and his boss, Inspector Yule, reported to headquarters G-section on January 19 that they were able to produce a readable printout from the duplicate tapes. They said G-section could select from several options the form in which they wanted to receive the printouts — by alphabetical sequence of names, by alphabetical sequence of occupations or by totals of political contributions by areas. "It is suggested that over the next two-three weeks you give consideration to what types of reports you require." A printout of names in alphabetical sequence was selected.

A voluminous printout of sheets sixteen inches by twelve inches and six feet high was produced. Only one copy was made. It was kept for more than three years in a special locked cabinet on the third floor at headquarters. No more than two Mounties had physical access to the Parti Québécois lists at any time. The combination to the cabinet lock was a closely held secret.

The McDonald Commission wanted to know what use was made of the lists and a number of Mountie witnesses were questioned on this point. Howard Draper said he couldn't recall any discussions about the use of the material prior to the raid. "First we would see what we had." There was the gnawing question of the large political contribution from a foreign source, of course, but the printouts didn't show anything of this nature. The records did, however, establish that a middle-level officer in the armed forces, whose loyalty was in question, was a contributor to the PQ. (Other witnesses said this officer was never charged with any offence.) From an intelligence point of view, Ham "supplied very, very little," Draper said.

Despite the denials, the McDonald Commission had the physical evidence of one of the early Ham Telex messages outlining the value of PQ lists to provide current information on separatist file subjects as well as information about "the degree of separatist infiltration of our key sectors—education, police and armed forces, and provincial and federal governments."

Draper said he instructed G-section chief J.E.A. Yelle and possibly Yelle's subordinate, Robert Potvin, that the lists weren't to be used in the routine security clearance screening of government employees and the names weren't to be put into the main Security Service index. "We weren't going to use it for any routine case. . . . The circle of knowledge that we possessed these things wasn't very great. . . . I didn't want to see this go into the regular system where anyone in the building with access to records could see it," Draper said. A log of the number of times G-section members might have consulted the printouts was never kept. The McDonald Commission was never able to determine with any certainty the extent to which the PQ lists were used. But the testimony of other witnesses indicates that such use occurred rarely.

Const. Robert Cadieux of headquarters G-section appears to have been the first custodian of the printouts. He received them from his immediate superior, Sergeant Potvin, and locked them in the cabinet next to his office. "I was the only one with the combination," Cadieux said. Potvin told Cadieux that nobody else was to see the printouts except Cadieux and then only when the request was approved by Potvin. Only twice was a request made and those were shortly after the final Ham break-in, Cadieux recalls. The first was a check to see if any members of the RCMP were listed. One name showed up listing the occupation as "federal policeman." On another occasion Potvin approved the request of Cpl. Yves Beaulieu of G-section in Montreal to check if one particular name was on the list. Cadieux found that it wasn't.

In the fall of 1973 Sgt. Bernie Limoges joined G-section at headquarters where he worked with Cadieux and Potvin. For several months he was aware of the locked cabinet near his office without knowing what it contained. He thought it was empty until one day he asked about it. Limoges was let in on the secret and he became the second Mountie who was allowed physical access to the printouts.

From that time until the Ham material was destroyed in 1975, according to Limoges there were less than a dozen approved requests to consult the printouts. These were simple checks to see if a name matched a name on the printouts. Knowledge that the printouts even existed was restricted to no more than four or five people in G-section. As a result, Limoges said, few even knew that this intelligence source was available. "The results of the operation were not what we anticipated . . . with the passage of time the lists became useless." Out of sheer curiosity he once checked to see if anyone with his family name was on the list.

In May 1974 Burnett was finishing up his duties with the force before taking a new job with the federal government. He turned over the Ham computer tapes, which were then placed in a registry file under the control of the Security Service. A memorandum for the Ham operational file was prepared by Hollas so that there would be a record of the location of this material to protect Burnett from anything "embarrassing should there be enquiries."

Meanwhile, the information from the Ham printouts showed up occasionally in reports as information from a source. Some Mounties not in on the secret thought this was a human source. Hollas was told in January 1975 that some of the G-section staff in Montreal wanted to interview this source. The confusion arose because the reports referred to the source with a general source number. Headquarters cleared this up by assigning the Ham printouts a specific number of its own, MC-685.

In late June 1975 Limoges recommended destroying the printouts and computer material because they were of little use and because of "our new mandate" from the government to quit spying on the Parti Québécois. (Prime Minister Trudeau told reporters after the Ham disclosure that the government put a halt to the spying on the PQ when he found out what the Security Service was up to. But he claimed that he never knew the extent of this spying activity nor that it included the theft of the computer tapes. The government, however, had been more than happy during the October Crisis when the RCMP and other police forces were able to come up with lists of people to be interned under the War Measures Act. The computer printouts could have become the ultimate list if there was a repeat of the October Crisis.)

Meanwhile, the CPIC computer staff conducted an inventory and noted that some Security Service computer tapes were being kept by the Security Service rather than in CPIC's "security shell" near the main computer rooms. This material included the PQ duplicate tapes. CPIC officials didn't know the nature of the material, but assumed it contained classified data.

Supt. J.G. Long, the officer in charge of CPIC, suggested that if the material wasn't needed any more his technicians would take care of it. "Our practice is to overwrite the data four times with alternating binary zeros and ones" to destroy the data, he wrote. The Security Service, however, felt that the Ham material was super-sensitive and had to be burned. Long was advised by Hollas on July 7 that "the content is extremely delicate and should any of this information fall into the wrong hands, it could prove embarrassing for the government as well as the RCMP...this type of information should not be out of the hands of the responsible authorities in the Security Service, because of the damaging effect it could have should they by accident or otherwise fall into the wrong hands." That same day Hollas gave one of his men a top secret memo ordering that the tapes and printouts be burned. Fridays were the one day each week when classified material was burned at the RCMP headquarters incinerator. In the early morning hours of Friday, July 18, Cpl. J.M. Dupuis gathered up the printouts from G-section and the tapes, put everything into three large cardboard boxes, and took it all down to the incinerator room. "I didn't see it physically destroyed. I left it there. It wasn't worth sticking around to see them burned because that would attract more attention," Dupuis said. But nothing ever came out of the incinerator room except ashes. Later that day the three boxes and their contents went up in smoke.

Like Operation Bricole (the break-in at the offices of a left-wing Montreal news agency) before it, Operation Ham was successfully covered up for years. In the case of Ham, however, the cover-up remained in place much longer. It was only after the creation of the McDonald Commission in July 1977 that an intensive investigation of Security Service activities uncovered Ham.

The PQ computer printouts and tapes became too hot to handle and were direct physical evidence of a break-in operation. Despite the official denials, however, it would have been entirely out of character for the Security Service to have failed to make more extensive use of the information obtained from Operation Ham than they claimed. The RCMP considered the PQ just as subversive in the early Seventies as it did the Communist party during the Thirties and Forties. Lists of Communist party members were used to open files on individuals. It would seem just as logical for the Security Service to use the PQ tapes to open files on separatist sympathizers previously unknown to the force and to merge the new information with existing files. When considering the elaborate lengths the force went to in obtaining the tapes it seems utterly illogical that the information wasn't used this way. Once files are opened it becomes almost impossible to determine whether the subject first came to the Security Service's attention as a result of Operation Ham, a tip from an informer or any other source of information. One can only speculate as to whether the names of hundreds of Québécois are now on file folders at RCMP headquarters because of Operation Ham.

6

The Cover-ups Crumble

Operation Bricole, Operation Ham and the other dirty tricks of the RCMP were among the most closely kept secrets within the force in 1974. Cover-ups were securely in place. The allegations of L'Agence de Presse Libre du Québec and Raymond Tremblay, the law student who was abandoned in the woods, were made publicly at press conferences. But they were denied or simply ignored by the authorities. The stories were buried on the back pages of newspapers and then forgotten. Mounties carried on with business as usual in the pretty safe belief that they were getting away with their misdeeds.

Staff Sgt. Don McCleery, however, found himself in trouble over other matters. He was fired from the force in December 1973 for allegedly having improper associations with people close to the Montreal underworld. McCleery felt he was fired unjustly. It was part of his job to develop contacts and sources and that might well mean getting to know people with underworld connections. Others from the old G-section fared better. There were promotions and career advancements for many. Don Cobb had been promoted to chief superintendent and was back in Montreal as head of the Security Service for the entire province.

The force was holding up pretty well during a Royal Commission's look at RCMP complaints procedures. The commission, headed by Judge René Marin, was supposed to examine the system employed by the RCMP in their investigations of complaints from citizens. Nobody in the force or in the solicitor-general's office told Judge Marin about the complaint lodged in 1972 by the APLQ.

The cover-up might have continued that way, perhaps forever, if it wasn't for the bad luck of Const. Robert Samson on a hot summer night in 1974—twenty-two months after he and other policemen broke into the APLQ offices. There has never been a satisfactory explanation of what Samson was doing on the night of July 26, 1974, outside the Town of Mount Royal home of Melvyn Dobrin, an executive with the Steinberg's Limited supermarket chain. Samson claims he was there on official business. He says that he received an anonymous phone tip from an informer who wanted to meet with him at the location, that there he spotted a parcel on the ground and when he bent down and touched it the package exploded in his face.

Three sticks of dynamite went off. Samson suffered burns and cuts to the front of his body. He lost the tips of four fingers on his left hand. His left eye was injured and he suffered a partial sight loss. The blast destroyed the hearing in his left ear. The explosion caused about $1,500 damage to the Dobrin house. Nobody inside was injured. Samson survived and was able to make his way to a hospital.

Samson had a friend call the Security Service to say that he had been injured repairing a car. A Mountie went to the hospital and spoke with Samson's doctor. From the description of the injuries it sounded as if Samson could have been involved in the Dobrin bomb blast. The Security Service informed Montreal police that Samson might know something about the explosion.

A Quebec fire commissioner's inquiry was held and Samson's story started to fall apart. He was charged with planting the bomb. The prosecution alleged that Samson had close links with Montreal underworld characters and implied that the bombing was part of an extortion plan that ended badly when the dynamite exploded prematurely. The first trial ended in mistrial. In the second in March 1976 the jury believed the prosecution's case and convicted Samson.

But there was another, totally unexpected outcome to the trial. It began when Samson was in the witness box testifying in his own defence. There was a legal question about the admissibility of some of the evidence and the jury was excused for a portion of the questioning. Samson testified that in his official RCMP duties he had done "much worse" things than plant a bomb. Crown prosecutor Jean Morin thought Samson was bluffing or was putting on a display of bravado. The lawyer was going to let the comment pass, but he tossed out a question anyway. "What?" Judge Peter Shorteno granted Samson the immunity of the Canada Evidence Act, the legal protection ensuring that whatever Samson was about to say couldn't be used in evidence against him in other legal proceedings that might result. Samson began to tell the story of Operation Bricole, the APLQ break-in.

"Let's say that at a certain time I committed a break and entry," Samson said. He named accomplices in the Montreal police, the Quebec Police Force and the RCMP. Judge Shorteno asked what this break-in was about. Samson said, "It was to take documents which were files of the most militant members as well as pertinent documents. L'Agence-Presse Libre always had a fairly big list of Quebec leftists." Samson said there were also "other things" done by police, but he couldn't remember them specifically. The cover-up had started to crumble. News reporters in the room knew that this was a big story. A Mountie had admitted that the APLQ's suspicions of a police break-in were not only correct, but also that three police forces were involved. But they had to sit on the story for several more weeks. Since Samson's revelations weren't directly relevant to the bombing case, the story wasn't repeated when the jury was brought back. To ensure fairness to Samson, Judge Shorteno ordered that the APLQ story not be reported until after the conclusion of the trial.

The RCMP didn't wait long to begin to prepare some kind of explanation for the break-in. Michael Dare, who had succeeded John Starnes as director-general of the Security Service, ordered Donald Cobb to prepare briefing material on the background of the caper. Cobb and his men made a lengthy written report on March 15. They acknowledged the truth of Samson's story. The language was brutally frank. It said the object of Operation Bricole was the "theft of records" from the Movement for the Defence of Political Prisoners of Quebec. "Illegal entry" was made. A "technical source" revealed the combination to the APLQ safe. The men in Montreal couldn't remember if they originally planned to copy the documents on the premises or whether the plan called for "stealing of the documents" all along. In discussions with the other forces it was decided that "stealing the documents" would so disrupt the MDPPQ that it would go out of business. The raid was described as an "illegal entry" and there was the hope that the "crime" would be blamed on the Milice Republicaine.

Dare didn't much like what he read. He wanted a report that he could give to Solicitor-General Allmand and the Quebec authorities who were responsible for criminal investigations in their province. He couldn't do much about the facts of the case, but he sent a top secret letter back to Cobb suggesting that the report could be "redrafted with the same factual accuracy, perhaps a bit shorter, with a language that would be more easily understood outside this force." Cobb got the hint. In the rewrite "theft of records" became "removal of records," "illegal entry" became "entry without warrant," "technical source"—a reference to a wiretap— became an "RCMP source," "stealing the documents" became "removing the documents" and "crime" became "loss."

Dare and other senior officers at headquarters contemplated several options. They discussed the possibility of recommending to Allmand that he reconvene the Marin Commission to investigate Samson's story. Another possibility was to resist an inquiry and stress to Allmand that Bricole was an isolated incident that could be investigated internally. Events were already getting out of hand, however.

Samson's trial concluded on March 30 and the break-in story was on the television news that night and in the papers the next morning. The PQ opposition in the Quebec National Assembly and the NDP and Tory opposition in the federal House of Commons were demanding explanations. Still with very little information to go on, Allmand told the Commons that "this raid was organized by either the Quebec provincial police or the Montreal police, and the RCMP assumed an assisting role."

It sounded to the Montreal and Quebec police that they were

being set up to take the rap. Cobb sent off a Telex to headquarters warning that if Allmand repeated that kind of statement it could "provoke a panic of recriminations that would have grave consequences far beyond the worst that can come of this affair."

Meanwhile, Quebec Attorney-General Fernand Lalonde said that he was starting an investigation. Each force was preparing its own report to Lalonde. Cobb was keeping his ear close to the ground to find out what line the other forces might try to take. On April 5 he reported to headquarters that the QPF and the Montreal police wanted Allmand to justify or "legitimize the Bricole affair as a matter of national security." The proposition was never seriously considered in Ottawa.

Lalonde's investigation resulted in Cobb, Insp. Jean Coutellier of the QPF and Insp. Roger Cormier of the Montreal police being charged with authorizing a search without a search warrant. The legal proceedings dragged into June 1977. All three officers pleaded guilty, thus ending any chance of a trial that might have exposed other Security Service operations or given a thorough airing of how the Bricole break-in had been covered up for so long.

But there was a newspaper reporter digging away at the cover-up angle. John Sawatsky of the *Vancouver Sun*'s Ottawa bureau spent months tracking down leads. He had information that senior officers at Security Service headquarters knew about Bricole within days of the break-in and that documents were taken from the raid to Ottawa where they were eventually destroyed. His biggest frustration was getting confirmation from second sources. And he was desperately trying to find Starnes, who seemed to have dropped from sight after his retirement as director-general. Then one day Sawatsky heard a radio report that John Starnes, former diplomat, was going to address an Ottawa civic group about foreign affairs. He reached an official of the group who gave him Starnes' address. Sawatsky couldn't believe it. Starnes was living in an apartment in an Ottawa high rise, just a few floors below Sawatsky's own apartment.

Sawatsky eventually got the confirmations he needed from the various sources he had carefully cultivated. On December 7, 1976, the *Vancouver Sun* ran Sawatsky's piece. The story, which later won the Michener Award for public service journalism, correctly reported for the first time that the cover-up extended all the way to the most senior ranks of the RCMP. To Sawatsky's dismay, the story produced little reaction east of the Rockies.

On June 17 Cobb, Coutellier and Cormier awaited their fate at the hands of Judge Roger Vincent. Cobb's lawyer, Pierre Lamontagne, pleaded convincingly that the three officers were upstanding policemen who had acted from the best of motives. They had tried to protect national security. It was only a momentary lapse when they'd authorized the raid without first obtaining a search warrant. It certainly wouldn't happen again, Lamontagne said. Judge Vincent granted all three unconditional discharges, a move that saved the men from incurring criminal records. The three officers returned to active duty.

With the criminal proceedings over, the new solicitor-general, Francis Fox, was free to discuss the case and answer the opposition's questions about how much his predecessor, Jean-Pierre Goyer, might have known about the APLQ. During his statement to the Commons, Fox said that the government had "repeated and unequivocal assurances from the RCMP that the APLQ incident was exceptional and isolated and that the directives of the RCMP to its members clearly require that all their actions take place within the law." Fox had been had and Don McCleery knew it. McCleery had been fighting his dismissal for more than three years. He was working as a Montreal private detective, but he still wanted to get back with the force and to clear his name. He had made earlier approaches to people in the solicitor-general's office. He thought the time had come to make another trip to Ottawa.

McCleery met with Deputy Solicitor-General Roger Tasse and Phillipe Landry, an assistant deputy minister in the Justice Department. He told the men that the APLQ was only the tip of the iceberg. The Security Service had been involved in other dirty operations and "it was the biggest cover-up since the blanket was invented." McCleery spoke in general terms: "I asked if opening mail was illegal, without going into specifics. I asked if possession of stolen dynamite was illegal, without going into specifics." McCleery told the two officials that if Fox had to answer any more questions in the Commons about the RCMP "he'd better be on his toes because if he thought that [the APLQ break-in] was an isolated incident, he was crazy."

When Fox learned of these new allegations he thought again of calling a Royal Commission to investigate. He ordered RCMP Commissioner Robert Simmonds to conduct some preliminary inquiries. Deputy Commissioner Raymond Quintal and Insp. Joseph Nowlan headed a team of internal investigators who started to sift through the old files of G-section. They discovered items such as the Dubé report describing the intimidation tactics that were employed in informer recruitment attempts. Former members of G-section were called in and told that they had to answer questioning or they would be charged with a major service offence under the RCMP Act for failure to obey an order to talk. McCleery's allegations about arson, dynamite theft and mail opening started to check out. Fox decided that there had to be a full-scale public inquiry.

On July 6—less than a month after saying that the APLQ affair was "exceptional and isolated"—Fox acknowledged in the House of Commons that that wasn't the case. New allegations had arisen that required a thorough investigation. The government, therefore, was establishing a Commission of Inquiry to be headed by Justice David C. McDonald of the Supreme Court of Alberta. His co-commissioners were lawyers Guy Gilbert of Montreal and Donald Rickerd of Toronto. The new commission's terms of reference were to investigate and to report on any instances of RCMP wrongdoing that might be brought to its attention. The APLQ break-in was mentioned specifically. But the commission was free to pursue any other allegations that might come up. Although the terms of reference didn't mention them specifically, the government told McDonald and his co-commissioners about McCleery's allegations. The commission had full subpoena powers and could order witnesses to testify. It could hire its own staff, including investigators, and its own lawyers. The commission, however, was to make its report to the government, not to Parliament, and the government would ultimately decide what portions of its final report would be made public. Furthermore, the commission was instructed to hold its hearings "in camera in all matters relating to national security and in all other matters where the commissioners deem it desirable in the public interest or in the interest of the privacy of individuals involved in specific cases which may be examined." In making its report, the commission was to protect the secrecy of Canadian sources of security information and foreign intelligence information provided to Canada by other countries. The policies and procedures of the RCMP could be examined and the investigation need not be limited to the Security Service.

Opposition MPs thought that the terms of reference were too restrictive. They wanted a public explanation of former Solicitor-General Jean-Pierre Goyer's possible involvement in the APLQ break-in. Nowhere in the terms of reference was there a mention of investigating the role of cabinet ministers. Fox said that the government felt that the terms of reference were very broad. Examining policies and procedures could include the policies and procedures of RCMP reporting to the solicitor-general's office. "The whole purpose of the Royal Commission cannot, by any stretch of the imagination, ever be conceived as a cover-up operation," Fox said.

The appointments stirred some initial cynicism. Judge McDonald had been involved in Liberal politics before his appointment to the bench. He served a term as president of the Liberal party in Alberta in 1966 and 1967. Gilbert had received some federal government legal work as a commission counsel in broadcasting-license applications to the Canadian Radio-Television and Telecommunications Commission. He was also concerned about the future of the Liberal party in Quebec after the election of the PQ and wrote to Le Devoir Editor Claude Ryan, urging him to seek the party leadership. Neither man made any secret of their past associations. The Globe and Mail made inquiries about McDonald's background and found that Alberta lawyers held the judge in high regard and praised him for his intelligence, integrity and thoroughness.

McDonald was a witty and urbane westerner. Born in Prince Albert, Saskatchewan, he was educated at the University of Alberta and at Oxford where he was a Rhodes Scholar. His law practice in Edmonton concentrated on civil litigation. As a judge his decisions were considered progressive. His mother started him on French lessons as a young boy and he improved his fluency after his appointment to the bench with lessons provided by the federal government.

Gilbert was an experienced courtroom lawyer who had pleaded six cases before the Supreme Court of Canada. His talent at cross-examination enabled him to get quickly to the heart of an issue. His questioning was frequently blunt and he often found it difficult to conceal his sentiments if he was displeased with the answer of a witness.

Rickerd was much like McDonald in temperament. He was slow to anger, but he wouldn't let a witness off the hook with a half answer. He was the president of the Donner Canadian Foundation, an endowed trust which provides research grants in the social sciences. He had taught history and law at York University and had practised law in Toronto before joining the foundation.

The McDonald Commission suffered some severe criticism for the slow, ponderous pace with which it started its work. There were rumours that fall that a federal election was imminent and a lot of journalists and opposition MPs suspected that the voting would be well over before Prime Minister Pierre Trudeau and his cabinet ministers would be called to account for their management of the RCMP. The new PQ government of Quebec had started its own provincial inquiry into G-section dirty tricks and it was making much more progress than the federal inquiry. The Quebec inquiry, headed by labour lawyer Jean Keable, was the hometown team in the minds of many Montreal journalists.

McDonald didn't seem to recognize, or perhaps wouldn't acknowledge, that his commission was starting out with a credibility problem. Comparisons with the Keable Commission were inevitable. Most of the RCMP dirty tricks known of at that time had occurred in Quebec and there was a general feeling in the province that the provincial inquiry had a better chance of getting to the bottom of things. Since the victims were anti-federalists there was a suspicion that a federal inquiry wouldn't be as tough on the federal police force. But McDonald was determined to be thorough. He had a judicial outlook on his commission's work— no outside influence would hasten or retard his pace. The risk was too great that by being hasty something might be overlooked.

McDonald was also having some practical problems. He wanted the best available team of lawyers and investigators. Finding them was difficult. Most of the best investigative talent was either in the RCMP or had been in the force. McDonald was conducting what amounted to a police investigation of crimes, but the suspects were all Mounties. He found the men he wanted as his two chief investigators in the Ontario Provincial Police and the Canadian armed forces. Staff Supt. John McKendry of the OPP was an experienced homicide investigator. He also had been in charge of the OPP's staff inspections branch, a unit responsible for internal investigations of allegations of police misconduct. Lt.-Col. Clifford Christian had been an RCMP constable for a short while before he joined the military in the early Fifties. During most of his military career he was a base security officer, the Canadian armed forces' equivalent of the police chief in a small town.

It took until October—four months after the creation of the McDonald Commission—to find a chief counsel. McDonald appointed John "Jake" Howard, a Toronto lawyer who had been a torpedo patrol boat commander during World War II. Howard had earned a reputation as a meticulous investigator of complex combines cases. He had the ability to examine thousands of documents and discover the common thread running through them. It was an ability that ideally suited him for investigating an organization like the RCMP which kept incredible amounts of documents about its activities. He also had been chief counsel for an Ontario provincial inquiry into contract irregularities in the construction of a Sudbury hospital. That inquiry resulted in the ousting of the hospital's board of trustees and criminal charges against some former officials. Howard was also a horse breeder, an avocation that resulted in some kidding about his being a "horseman"—a term Mounties sometimes use to describe themselves. His secret passion was to someday meet the real life counterpart of George Smiley, the fictional agent of British intelligence in the spy novels of John le Carré. Howard and McDonald put together a formidable stable of commission lawyers to deal with specific aspects of the investigation.

Ross Goodwin of Quebec City was a devastating cross-examiner. He and Yvon Tarte, a bright young Ottawa lawyer, put together the case on informer-recruiting tactics. John Sopinka and Tony Kelly of Toronto made sense out of mountains of paper in the cases of RCMP access to supposedly confidential income tax and unemployment insurance records. The commission from time to time employed two of the most respected courtroom lawyers in Montreal, A.J. Campbell and Bruno Pateras.

The RCMP had some considerable legal talent to represent the interests of members of the force. Pierre Lamontagne, who had represented Cobb at his trial, was in charge of the RCMP's case. He had a sharp legal mind and the ability to think quickly on his feet. The day-to-day proceedings were handled by a younger lawyer, Richard Mongeau of Montreal.

Representing the federal cabinet and the office of the solicitor-general were Joseph Nuss and Michel Robert, considered by their colleagues to be among the best lawyers in Quebec. Assisting them with the daily chores was Allan Lutfy, a talented young man who went on to become a personal aide to Trudeau.

On the rare occasions when all of the lawyers were assembled at one time in the hearing room they made an impressive array.

McDonald spent much of his time in the first few months researching the law concerning the powers of a commission of inquiry. He studied precedents in Britain and other Commonwealth countries. He also began to amass literature about the role of security agencies in the U.S. and elsewhere. The commission later hired a research director, Peter Russell, an academic from the University of Toronto, who prepared such a complete issues paper on the role of the RCMP that it has been used in law school classes.

There were logistics problems. Office and support staff had to be hired. Because they would have access to classified documents they had to have security clearances. Office space had to be found in Ottawa and an office opened in Toronto because Howard did a lot of commission work there when he couldn't get away from his law practice. McDonald hired Harry Johnson, a Victoria lawyer, to serve as the commission's executive secretary and to handle the logistics. The offices had to be fitted out with safes and new door locks to ensure the protection of classified material. Guy Robitaille, a former military security officer, was hired as the commission's security officer. Bill Brennan, who had been a registrar at another Royal Commission, was hired as the McDonald Commission's registrar to keep track of the hundreds of exhibits and to make sure news reporters got copies of documents as they were declassified.

While the McDonald Commission was working quietly in preparation for public hearings, the RCMP story was continuing to break elsewhere. Senior editors at the *Globe and Mail* were convinced that there was much more to be learned about the operations of the Security Service. Lawrence Martin was assigned to the story full time. Starting from scratch, Martin developed sources who knew a lot about what had gone on but were afraid to talk publicly. Elaborate precautions were taken to make certain that contacts with the reporter remained secret. Months of work finally produced stories revealing that the RCMP had spied on the NDP and had used confidential medical records to discredit so-called subversives. The *Globe* assigned other reporters to develop leads. John Marshall and I beat the bushes in Ottawa and Richard Cleroux, the Montreal bureau chief, pumped his contacts in that city.

In late October Fox made public Operation Ham, the PQ break-in. In November the CBC exposed mail-opening operations and Operation 300, the code name for break-ins. That same month the Keable Commission first learned of the barn-burning episode and the dynamite theft. A new, fictionalized account of the Security Service was published as a novel. But some of the characters and events seemed to so closely parallel real life that the book set off a new set of rumours about dirty tricks. There were other rumours, never confirmed, that the RCMP had a file containing highly embarrassing information about the private lives of important people in Ottawa. So many of the amazing stories had already been confirmed that almost any rumour, no matter how fantastic, seemed possible. Dissent was showing up in cabinet ranks. One cabinet minister, Monique Begin, criticized the government's handling of the RCMP affair at a public meeting at Carleton University. She then tried to deny she had made the remarks until a tape recording was produced. Opposition MPs were pounding away daily in the Commons, demanding explanations from the government. Trudeau and his ministers ducked the questions by saying everything was being investigated by the McDonald Commission. Events were proceeding at such a pace that Jake Howard commented: "I wake up each morning and listen to the seven o'clock news and I hear that we have a new problem."

Meanwhile, the Keable Commission was having its problems with the federal government. Keable wanted to see RCMP and government documents from the files in Ottawa. He was trying to determine the chain of responsibility and possible criminal culpability from G-section in Montreal up to the top. Since the provinces have jurisdiction over criminal investigations and prosecutions, Keable had clear legal authority to investigate criminal acts that might have occurred in Quebec. But Keable was demanding to see things like the operational manuals for the Security Service and written correspondence that might exist concerning reports to the solicitor-general on the APLQ break-in. The federal government said Keable was overstepping the bounds and was getting into areas of national security, a federal responsibility. Fox refused to comply with Keable's subpoenas and used provisions of the Federal Court Act to block the production of documents. Keable threatened contempt action. A classic constitutional fight ensued. The wrangle ended up in the courts where it dragged on, unresolved for months. Regardless of the legal merits of the federal government's case, it seemed that Fox and the cabinet had something they wanted to hide. The absence of any public sign of life from the McDonald Commission added to the suspicions that nobody would ever get to the bottom of the key issue of ministerial responsibility for the RCMP.

When the McDonald Commission opened its first set of public hearings in December in Montreal it was faced with its first procedural hurdle. Civil liberties groups and the federal Progressive Conservative party wanted the right to have lawyers present and the right to cross-examine witnesses. The civil liberties groups argued that they wanted their lawyers to represent the public interest. The commission denied the request, saying that representing the public interest was the job of Jake Howard and the other commission lawyers.

Then there was the question of how much of the proceedings

should be heard in public. McDonald, Rickerd and Gilbert all favoured as much openness as possible. They recognized that some evidence might have to be heard in camera because of legitimate national security concerns. But they promised that these would be minimal. The whole point of the inquiry, they said, was to let the public know what was going on inside the RCMP. Over the months RCMP and government lawyers raised numerous objections to certain evidence being heard in public and the commission had to make a number of rulings. In most instances the commission couldn't find a legitimate reason for keeping information secret. One of the RCMP objections, if sustained, could have cut off public disclosure of many of the RCMP's activities. The RCMP argued that it wasn't in the public interest to reveal police investigative techniques. The commission ruled that it wouldn't agree to keep secret the police techniques that were illegal.

The federal government's court fight with the Keable inquiry brought that commission's work to a standstill. The Supreme Court eventually ruled that it could resume, but with much narrower terms of reference. The McDonald Commission soon caught up and passed the point where the Keable inquiry had left the APLQ break-in. And the federal inquiry explored whole new avenues of investigation in the mail-opening and the use of confidential files cases. The hearings were thorough, sometimes painfully so, and they were slow going. The first round of witnesses were low- or middle-ranking members of the force. It took almost ten months to get to the point where the commission lawyers felt they were ready to question cabinet ministers and former senior officials, such as Higgitt and Starnes. And then, in an abrupt about-face, the federal government lawyers wanted to change the rules of the game.

In October 1978, just days before the scheduled appearance of the senior officials and politicians, the government discovered the doctrine of cabinet privilege. As Nuss and Robert argued it, the government itself would decide what evidence could be heard in public about communications between ministers and their civil servants and among the various ministers. It sounded an awful lot like the executive privilege argument advanced by former U.S. President Richard Nixon to try to hang on to the Watergate tapes.

Cabinet privilege could be invoked to effectively cut off any public disclosure of possible wrongdoing by the politicians.

A storm of editorial protest broke over the heads of Trudeau and his solicitors-general, past and present. Editorial writers quickly latched onto the Watergate comparison and smelled the possibility of cover-up. The credibility of the McDonald Commission was on the line. McDonald, Rickerd and Gilbert had won the confidence of many of the initial skeptics because they had been so thorough and independent. And now, would they back down?

The McDonald Commission stubbornly refused to back away from the confrontation. On October 13 it issued its answer, a lengthy reaffirmation of its independence and its own authority to decide what would be heard in public. And if the government didn't like that, then cabinet would have to change the commission's terms of reference with a formal order-in-council. The McDonald Commission's decision cited Watergate legal precedents in the U.S. At almost the same moment as McDonald was reading the decision to a packed hearing room, Trudeau was talking to a high-school assembly on the other side of town. In response to a question by a student, Trudeau said, "I don't think the public has a right to know everything," and that the government, not the commission, would ultimately decide what would be made public.

The government was pitting itself against a commission that had more public credibility than it did. To have formally changed the terms of reference or to have challenged the commission's ruling in court could have had politically disastrous consequences for the Liberals. It might have provoked the resignations of the commissioners. The government backed away and the commission went on with its work.

7

Operation Cathedral

Canada has one of the toughest mail-tampering laws in the world. The law's antiquated toughness is illustrated by the provision that a toll-gate keeper can't halt or delay a mail truck even if the driver refuses to pay the toll. The Post Office Act says: "Notwithstanding anything in any other Act or law, nothing is liable to demand, seizure or detention while in the course of post...." The Post Office Act makes very few exceptions—customs inspections of parcels from abroad and Post Office seizure of explosives in the mail. By the very wording of the act—"notwithstanding... any other Act or law"—police are forbidden from using Criminal Code search and seizure warrants to intercept mail or open it.

The RCMP has been breaking the Post Office Act for longer than anyone in the force can remember—at least twenty-five years and maybe closer to forty years. The Mounties knew it was illegal. But they took great care that they wouldn't get caught. On the Security Service side of the force, mail tampering became so institutionalized that it was eventually given a code name— Operation Cathedral. Judge McDonald said at one point he wanted to find out how Cathedral might have started as a "wee church," but the origin of the code name remained obscure. There were three varieties of Cathedral operations. Cathedral A was a "mail cover check," or letter interception, to obtain names and addresses from an envelope. Cathedral B involved photographing or photocopying the envelope. Cathedral C meant opening mail to get at the contents and then carefully resealing the envelope. The Security Service targets for Cathedral operations ranged from the suspected contacts for terrorists to alleged foreign espionage agents. But the McDonald Commission didn't press for any great public disclosure of the backgrounds of the targets and there was little way of knowing how many totally innocent people might have had their mail tampered with. The Criminal Investigations Branch also opened mail. In most cases, these openings were for the purpose of searching for drugs. The CIB didn't have any code name for this kind of operation.

The RCMP covered up its mail-tampering activities, lied about them, permitted cabinet ministers to make misleading statements in the House of Commons, and recruited Post Office employees as accomplices in crime. When they got caught, the Mounties didn't express any regret or remorse. They didn't agree to tell who in the Post Office helped them tamper with mail. Instead, they put on a public relations campaign to try to convince the public, Parliament and the McDonald Commission that they should be allowed to tamper with mail—that the fault was not with the RCMP, but with the law. And they got the federal government to agree.

The centrepiece of the public relations campaign was a true life thriller from the files of the Security Service. It was a brilliant anti-terrorist operation which ended successfully with the arrest of a member of the Japanese Red Army. Prime Minister Pierre Trudeau and the Mounties said that here was a case that showed just how important mail-opening authority is for the RCMP. But when the McDonald Commission got down to questioning the RCMP participants it turned out that the terrorist had been caught by conventional means, a legal wiretap.

The Japanese Red Army was the scourge of Western security and intelligence agencies throughout the early and mid-1970s. An extremely violence-prone anti-Zionist Marxist group, the JRA was responsible for the Lod Airport massacre in Israel in 1972.

Twenty-six people, including two of the terrorists, were killed. In Japan, the JRA had been responsible for several bombings. The organization had grown out of the student protest movement at Japanese universities and expanded its field of operations across the globe. In 1975 its members had staged armed takeovers of foreign embassies in The Hague and Kuala Lumpur. It hadn't been active in North America, although at least one of the participants in the Lod massacre had travelled through Canada on the way to Israel. Kyoto police also suspected that JRA financing was linked to the Black Panthers and drugs in the United States. The Kyoto police believed Toshio Omura, the man the Mounties caught, acted as a hemp and LSD courier between the U.S. and Japan.

The RCMP uncovered evidence that two JRA members had attended a Montreal conference in support of Palestinians in 1970. The evidence was in the form of a letter found in the possession of an illegal immigrant in Montreal who was deported. The letter was from T. Hatano, the assumed name of a JRA member. It thanked the illegal immigrant for allowing the two JRA members to stay with him during the conference. "I would like to keep the really revolutionary solidarity with you ... and the Quebec War people," Hatano wrote. (It seems likely that Hatano mistook the word Québécois for Quebec War.) There was also a promise to send along a publication containing the plans for the hijacking of an "imperialist plane." The letter concluded: "Please take care of yourself and your struggle. All Power to the People! Right On!" And there was a postscript. "Please burn out this letter for our security."

Staff Sgt. James Pollock was the senior noncommissioned officer in charge of the international terrorism desk at headquarters. He had the JRA very much on his mind since he was involved in planning the security for the 1976 Montreal Olympic Games. Like Expo 67 almost a decade earlier, the Olympics would focus world attention on Montreal and Canada and could provide an international stage for terrorists. There was the grisly precedent of the 1972 Olympics in Munich where Palestinian terrorists forced their way into the athletes' compound and killed members of the Israeli team.

In early September 1975 authorities in Sweden rounded up two suspected Japanese terrorists and deported them to Japan. Just about the same time Canadian authorities arrested and deported a third Japanese wanted for terrorist acts in his home country. On September 11 a Japanese Red Army spokesman in Damascus issued a warning to Canadian, Swedish and Japanese "imperialists" to expect bloody retribution. "We warn [the countries] ... you did not learn your lesson from the operations in The Hague and Kuala Lumpur. It looks as though you are begging for more lessons." The warning was carried internationally on the wires of the Reuter news agency, but it didn't come to the attention of the Security Service until the story was spotted in a Swedish newspaper by an RCMP liaison officer attached to the Canadian embassy in Stockholm.

Also that fall West German security authorities tipped off the Mounties that they had found the address of a Toronto resident in the address book of Shinji Omura, Toshio's younger brother. Shinji was believed to be a relay and contact for JRA communications. The Toronto man, a Japanese citizen, was never identified publicly at the McDonald Commission because he is the subject of a continuing investigation. But Pollock said that when the Security Service unit in Toronto began the investigation it was quickly determined that the Toronto man and his wife were legal landed immigrants who had been in Canada for two years. The Mounties could get very little additional information. On Christmas Eve, 1975, the Security Service in Toronto asked headquarters for approval of "Cathedral C coverage" — the code name for mail opening. They wanted to open the Toronto man's mail from January 5 to January 31. On December 29 headquarters Telexed back that Cathedral C was denied "at this time," but that approval was given for Cathedral B — mail interception and photocopying of envelope covers. Cathedral B coverage approval was eventually extended to the end of May. On January 14 the Security Service applied for and received the approval of Solicitor-General Warren Allmand to tap the telephone of the Toronto man. The approval was granted under Section 16 of the Official Secrets Act, which permits the interception of private communications to detect "subversive activity." It took several days for the wiretap to be installed.

Security Service officers in Toronto were impatient to find out who the Toronto man might be talking to on the phone. On January 22, in direct violation of the Post Office Act and orders, they opened the man's telephone bill for the previous month. It didn't seem to occur to them that they could have quite legally obtained the same information from Bell Canada records. As it turned out, Pollock said, the phone bill showed no long distance charges of any interest to the Security Service.

In February the Cathedral B mail-cover checks showed that the Toronto man and his wife received a money order from abroad for $768. Pollock said this was discovered because it was easy to see through the envelope. Furthermore, a check with foreign intelligence sources showed that the sender's husband had recently "defected to an Eastern Block" country.

On April 8 the Toronto man received a registered letter from West Germany from a "Joe." Joe was the alias of Toshio Omura. Four days later the cobra source wiretap revealed that the Toronto man's wife made enquiries at the University of Toronto about admission of foreign students to the economics program. The next day the Toronto couple posted a bulky brown envelope to Joe. The couple was under physical surveillance and the Mounties moved in and intercepted the envelope after it was dropped in a mail box. The Toronto investigators thought this envelope might contain plans for where and when Omura would enter Canada. Again, in violation of orders, they opened it. All they found were two blank university application forms. Toronto reported to headquarters that there was "no doubt" that the envelope contained admission forms. But Toronto didn't say that this certainty was the result of actually opening the mail. Toronto falsified its report to Ottawa, reporting that "tests were conducted re thickness of U of T application forms..." and they matched. Headquarters apparently bought the story or suspected the worst and didn't ask questions. The mail opening didn't tell the Mounties anything they didn't already know—that the Toronto couple was in touch with Omura and there were some plans for a foreign student to enter the University of Toronto. It seemed reasonable to assume that Omura would soon be coming to Canada as a student.

On the very day that the bulky brown envelope was opened, Michael Dare, the director-general of the Security Service, wrote to Solicitor-General Warren Allmand seeking permission to open the mail to and from the Toronto couple. Dare told Allmand that a "reliable confidential source" reported that the Toronto man was "intensively studying the revolutionary handbook, *The Trembling Clock,* which contains, among other instructions to the urban guerrilla, information and diagrams on the construction of explosive devices." The Toronto man also talked about his support of and involvement with the "simultaneous revolution"—a JRA slogan. Dare mentioned the letter from Joe. The return address was known to West German authorities as "the nest"—a gathering place for "militant left-wing radicals." Dare said the Security Service had enough evidence to get a warrant and move in to search the Toronto man's home. But this would tip the Mounties' hand and Omura would just find another way to get into Canada, perhaps with the help of another contact who was unknown to the force. Instead, Dare wanted Allmand to agree with the RCMP interpretation of the Official Secrets Act and authorize interception of mail communications. One week later Allmand signed a warrant authorizing mail openings. Allmand and the RCMP say that the warrant was never put into effect because Allmand insisted on getting a Justice Department legal opinion and Justice's lawyers said this would be a Post Office Act violation. But Allmand didn't wait for the opinion before signing the warrant and the cancellation stamp on the warrant was dated December 15, 1976—almost nine months after the warrant was signed.

The wiretap continued to give the Mounties further evidence that the Toronto man was in contact with both Omuras throughout the summer months. But the Olympics passed without incident or any sign of Toshio Omura's presence in Canada. Allmand's wiretap authorization continued until the end of the year so the Mounties continued to monitor the Toronto man's phone calls throughout the fall. Unbeknownst to the Mounties at the time, Toshio Omura flew into Montreal from Germany on December 4. He used a forged passport. Two days later he was in Toronto and visited the couple. The Mounties discovered Omura's presence because of the wiretap. The watcher service began twenty-four-hour surveillance of Omura. They followed him so closely that they were able to see the address he wrote on an envelope when he went to a post office to mail it. The Japanese authorities were notified. He was wanted there on a bombing charge. The plan was to arrest him and quickly deport him to Japan. But the Japanese didn't want to take him unless they could be supplied with positive proof that the man the Mounties were following was really Omura. The RCMP was reluctant to move in and make the arrest until the force was sure it could get Omura out of the country quickly. The Mounties feared that if they held Omura in a Canadian jail for any length of time the word would get back to other JRA members. The JRA might then try to stage a terrorist act, perhaps a plane hijacking, in an attempt to win Omura's release. The watchers were extremely good at their job. They never lost sight of their target during eight days of tailing. They followed Omura to the Japanese consulate in Toronto on several occasions. Omura read Japanese newspapers at the consulate, but the Security Service suspected that he might also be casing the building in preparation for a bombing.

Allmand and Immigration Minister Bud Cullen were kept informed of the progress of the investigation. On December 10 Cullen signed a warrant for Omura's arrest. The warrant was under the power of a special immigration bill, in force only during the Olympic year. The law severely restricted the right to appeal a deportation order. So the Mounties were facing a deadline if they were going to hustle Omura out of the country after a quick arrest. The special deportation powers expired December 31. The watchers thought they had the evidence they needed at one point when they followed Omura to a restaurant. When Omura left, one of his tails stayed behind and got the coffee cup which Omura had used. It was rushed to the laboratory for fingerprint analysis. Unfortunately the prints were smudged and inconclusive. Sometime later the watchers got the break they had been waiting for. Omura visited a bookstore and picked up a volume wrapped in cellophane. Omura left the store without buying the book. But the watchers bought it. This time the laboratory got clear prints and positive proof for the Japanese that the target was Omura. Insp. Randil Claxton took charge of the final stage of the planning.

Timing was important. There could be no delays. Airline sched-
ules to Japan were checked and seats booked. On December 14
the Mounties, armed with an arrest warrant and a search warrant, raided a Toronto apartment where Omura was staying. Omura was arrested and on a plane on his way to Japan before he
knew what happened to him. In the search the Mounties found
Omura had a doctored passport in a phoney name and an address
book with Canadian addresses. The addresses were written in
code. They also found a cryptic letter, which said in part: "Please
replace the address number JWI with JSGII. So,
KKZWZWPSEWYPNJI is just. It's all." RCMP cryptograph experts are still trying to figure that one out.

The Omura case was a textbook example of a successful anti-
terrorist operation, but the members of the McDonald Commission were puzzled as to why the RCMP thought it demonstrated
that they needed mail-opening authority. Commissioner Guy
Gilbert said that with the benefit of hindsight it seemed that the
end result would have been the same even without opening the
phone bill and the university application forms envelope. Pollock, the case officer from headquarters, agreed that if the Security
Service had known that the cobra wiretap was going to be as
useful as it was "we could have dispensed with" the mail openings.

The same sort of admission was harder to get from Inspector
Claxton. His testimony came after Pollock's, and Claxton's effort
seemed to be an attempt to salvage things for the Mounties.
"Cathedral operations were one investigative aspect [of the Omura case] . . . but a very vital one," Claxton said. He revealed that
in addition to the two mail openings there were inspections of the
covers of twenty-three envelopes addressed to Omura's Toronto
contact. Cover checks aren't necessarily illegal as long as the mail
isn't detained or diverted. But throughout his testimony Claxton
failed to distinguish between the Cathedral B cover checks and
the two clearly illegal Cathedral C mail openings. The Cathedral B
cover checks might well have been vital to establish the link between Toshio (Joe) Omura and the Toronto man, but not the
openings. Claxton finally conceded that point when he was interviewed by reporters after his testimony.

Claxton told the commission that without the link established by the "Cathedral operations" the wiretap which eventually revealed Omura's presence in Toronto would have been dropped. Judge McDonald reminded Claxton that there was no need to drop the wiretap because the authorization ran until the end of the year. Well, it was a matter of priorities, Claxton said. There wasn't enough wiretapping equipment to go around. Commission member Rickerd zeroed in on this and said that the argument for the need of mail-opening authority really came down to a management question of allocating resources in this particular case.

The Omura story was quite interesting, but as the centrepiece of the public relations drive to sell mail openings it was a bust.

Nobody was ever able to determine when RCMP mail-tampering operations began. Postmaster-General Jean-Jacques Blais, who later became solicitor-general, said that postal staff cooperated with the Mounties on mail interceptions as early as 1954. Murray Sexsmith, a deputy director-general of the Security Service, knew that the force was lobbying the government for mail-opening authority in 1939. There were few records kept at headquarters prior to 1970 when the Security Service centralized its Cathedral operations.

The earliest relevant document unearthed by the McDonald Commission was a 1952 memo from the Post Office's director of administration to local postmasters. It suggests that postmasters were taking their obligations under the Post Office Act very seriously. The memo says postmasters were erroneously assuming that they couldn't provide police with any information about patrons or former patrons "even though they have personal knowledge which would assist police officers." The memo reminded them that the postmasters couldn't divulge information "obtained as a result of . . . handling mail" or possessing Post Office records. But postmasters, in their capacity as private citizens, were at liberty to assist police. And the director of administration found it necessary to remind postmasters that they had an obligation to report robberies to police. But "not under any circumstances" was mail to be detained or given to anyone other than the addressee.

The rules started to be relaxed, just slightly, in 1956. The Treasury Board informed the Post Office that it was to cooperate with other government departments in trying to track down people who owed the government money. District postal inspectors were to provide forwarding addresses for tax delinquents or other deadbeats who were trying to skip out on bills they owed to Ottawa.

On the unofficial level individual Mounties developed their own cooperative sources within local post offices. The degree of cooperation depended to a large extent on how well the postal staff and the Mounties got on together personally and on the chances of getting caught.

In 1961 Parliament gave the Mounties extraordinary search and seizure powers under the Narcotics Control Act. With their writs of assistance — super search warrants — certain designated Mounties had the power to go anywhere in Canada at any time and search any place where they reasonably believed drugs might be found. There was no need to get a separate warrant for each search. This new development caused postal officials to review their own position. But in March 1962 regional postal inspectors and directors were instructed that the Post Office Act took precedence and overrode the Narcotics Control Act. Mail in the course of post was still immune from search and seizure.

However, the directive said that postal officials could cooperate with the RCMP to the extent of telling the Mounties when and where parcels suspected of containing narcotics were to be delivered. The trick, of course, was in trying to determine what parcels might contain drugs. It was up to the Mounties to come up with that information on their own. When they did they were able to get postal officials to help with "controlled deliveries" of drug parcels. The Mounties would wait in hiding until the letter carrier delivered the parcel and then they'd move in. The Mounties sometimes went further. They dressed up in the uniforms of letter carriers and delivered the parcels themselves. As soon as the addressee accepted the parcel he would be subject to a search and arrest. The 1962 directive gave local postal officials a free hand to decide for themselves what help they might give to the Mounties. "Considering the varying circumstances under which the Royal Canadian Mounted Police may request our assistance, it is difficult to describe the procedure to be followed, but we rely on the good judgment of our senior officers in the field to exercise discretion in all cases.... Reports of action taken in matters relating to this directive are not required at headquarters." In effect, the senior officials of the Post Office told their local officials to make up their own minds as to how much help to give the RCMP, but to use discretion. And Ottawa didn't want to know about it.

In 1965 officials in the Department of Justice came up with an interpretation of the Post Office Act that would prevent delivery of mail if it was known to contain narcotics. Justice said that such parcels could be interpreted to be mail "the delivery of which is prohibited by law." This made the drug parcels "undeliverable mail" under the Post Office Act and they had to be sent to the dead letter office, the place that also gets the letters to Santa Claus. But the Justice Department warned that postal officials had to know for sure that the parcels contained narcotics—they couldn't open them to find out.

From a law enforcement point of view the dead letter dope proposal wasn't much use at all. Even if the Mounties could convince the Post Office that a certain parcel contained narcotics, the only thing that could be done was to stop its distribution. It couldn't be used as evidence to arrest and convict the drug dealers. Controlled deliveries remained the favoured way of dealing with drugs sent through the mail.

During this same period senior Post Office officials issued a policy statement to postal inspectors aimed at cementing good relations with the police. It said, in part, "Considering the varying circumstances in which police may request assistance it is not possible to lay down an exact set of rules.... It is expected however that [postal] investigators will always exercise discretion and good judgment when complying with these requests." The policy added that "it is important in the interests of friendly cooperation that every investigator establish a good relationship with the police in his own area of responsibility." This last part was easy enough. Many of the postal inspectors were former Mounties. The policy statement didn't include a reminder about the mail-tampering prohibitions in the Post Office Act. In effect, it advocated flexibility and discretion. It was an open invitation to violate the Post Office Act.

By 1970 the Security Service's mail-tampering Cathedral operations were such standard fare that a formalized two-page policy for violating the Post Office Act was written at headquarters and issued to the field units. Howard Draper, the former deputy director-general, told the McDonald Commission that procedures requiring headquarters approval were adopted in 1970 because "it seemed there were many opportunities for excessive use. . . . Somebody might be going to take the easy way out and follow a line of least resistance." The policy document is written in Security Service argot. But Draper, who wrote the document, interpreted it for the McDonald Commission. It said that mail interceptions and openings were an extremely important source of information, especially in counterespionage cases. But men in the field were getting careless and "unconsciously exposing this source's availability to unwarranted risk." The units were reminded "that any form of cooperation received from any Cathedral source is contrary to existing regulations." Draper said that meant that post office employees helping to intercept mail were breaking the law. But, the memo said, "Since these investigations involve National Security it is considered there is a sufficient element of justification to proceed with the development and cultivation of sources who are willing to cooperate on this basis." Draper said the Security Service found Post Office employees who were willing to help. The Security Service, he said, didn't want to force anyone to cooperate against his will. "The individual would have to be comfortable with the request. We would want them to do it out of the goodness of their heart." Draper and other RCMP witnesses wouldn't identify their accomplices by name or position within the Post Office.

The memo says, "Each source who cooperates with the force is actually risking his livelihood and this fact must be kept in mind when the individual is being recruited and subsequently handled." Judge McDonald noted that not only were Post Office employees risking their jobs, they were also risking going to prison.

The memo outlined a complicated security precaution to prevent the identity of the Post Office employees from becoming known. It said, "In the future Cathedral sources must not be openly identified by name when submitting information or documents which were obtained through them. Similarly, the code name Cathedral or this file number (D 938-Q-22) should not be used to identify the source. This code name exists only to describe the type of coverage under discussion on the particular operational file." The Security Service is very secretive about its sources. It figures, with a fair amount of justification, that people will stop providing them with information if there is a chance that their identities might become known some day. Code numbers are assigned and used in operation reports that might be seen internally by a fairly large group of Mounties. The actual names are matched up with the numbers only in very few documents and these documents can be seen by only a very limited number of people within the Security Service.

The memo said the new precautions were being established to maintain security as tight as that for "Panther, Vampire and Cobra" sources, the code names for break-in, bugging and wiretap operations. Information from mail tamperings was often needed by other operational branches and the memo set out procedures for coordinating these efforts. There was also to be liaison with staff from the Criminal Investigations Branch "to ensure there is no conflict. We believe such precautions are necessary since indiscretion anywhere could have national implications which would jeopardize the utilization of this source across Canada."

The field units were advised that when they requested permission for a Cathedral operation they should specify the type: Cathedral A, "routine name or address check"; Cathedral B, "intercept but do NOT open"; or Cathedral C, "intercept and attempt content examination." Cathedral A and B operations could be authorized at the field level by the local officer in charge or one of his designated officers. But "because of the special experience required to handle Cathedral C, and for this reason alone" mail openings had to be approved by the office of the director-general. Permission would be granted, it stated, "contingent on the importance of the case and the availability of a trained technician."

The memo was written by Draper and sent out by Asst. Commissioner L.R. Parent, one of Starnes' deputies, on November 2, 1970. Starnes said he never saw the memo because he was at home ill at the time it was issued. Furthermore, in his entire time as director-general nobody ever told him that his men were involved in mail openings. Parent couldn't be called to testify. *Globe and Mail* reporter John Marshall discovered Parent was the victim of a medical disorder which produced memory loss.

Starnes testified that if he hadn't been ill with pneumonia the memo would have been brought to his attention. He would have been "upset and worried about the risk my people were taking," and he would have gone to Prime Minister Trudeau with the problem. Starnes may have heard the code name Cathedral, but he didn't know its meaning; he might have seen intelligence reports that were based on information obtained from Cathedral operations. But because of the tight security, most intelligence reports were drafted in such a way that the uninitiated reader wasn't given any clue as to the source of the information. Phrases such as "a source" or "a reliable source" were used to mask the use of mail tamperings or wiretaps. An uninformed reader might think the report was talking about a human source. Starnes said that the extent of his knowledge was that with the help of people in the Post Office the Security Service had access to information from the covers of envelopes.

In 1969 a Royal Commission report on national security recommended that the Security Service be given the legal authority to open mail with a proper warrant. The edited portions of the report which were made public gave no hint that the Royal Commission ever knew that the RCMP was already opening mail. Starnes said he urged the government to act on the recommendation, but nothing ever came of it.

Former Commissioner Higgitt, however, says that various solicitors-general must have known that the Security Service was opening mail. The ministers were seeing reports that clearly indicated that information was coming either from opening letters or from people who had X-ray vision. The ministers have all denied this. What's more, former Solicitor-General Warren Allmand says that he asked specifically and was told that the force didn't open mail.

This lie was passed on to a member of Parliament, Allan Lawrence, because of a curious series of events. In the spring of 1973 Wally Keeler, a Cobourg, Ontario, man, noticed that he wasn't getting some of his mail. Keeler was a member of a group known as the People's Republic of Poetry and he was used to getting some interesting letters from his friends in the group. The People's Republic of Poetry was a loosely organized circle of friends and acquaintances who sent each other poems dealing with the Orwellian *1984* view of the state. They were basically civil libertarians who took pleasure in spoofing the depersonalization associated with things like Social Insurance Numbers and postal codes. The poets called each other language technicians, or langteks for short. In correspondence they identified each other by Social Insurance Number rather than by name. Keeler thought somebody in authority somewhere might be intercepting his mail. He devised an experiment to test his theory.

A plasticized computer card was made up in the form of a postcard. One of Keeler's friends in Pembroke mailed it to Keeler. It was addressed: Langtek, followed by Keeler's Social Insurance Number and his address, 23 Chapel Street, Cobourg, Ontario, K9A 1N7. The message typed on the card read: "UNAUTHORIZED PERSONNEL HAVE BEEN SCANNING SENSITIVE INFORMATION AND RECORDING SAME FOR UNKNOWN REASON." Proper postage was affixed and the card was posted on July 19. The Pembroke Post Office sorted it properly and sent it on to the regional processing plant in Ottawa. Somebody there spotted it and turned it over to the Department of National Defence. Shortly thereafter Keeler's friend in Pembroke was questioned by the RCMP about the card and the People's Republic of Poetry. The Mounties thought it might be some subversive group.

When Keeler learned of this he sought the help of a Cobourg lawyer. The lawyer called the Mounties to complain. An investigation was promised. Keeler also went to his local MP, Tory Allan Lawrence. Lawrence raised the issue with Solicitor-General Allmand. Allmand asked the Mounties what it was about and that they prepare a reply for Lawrence. The Mounties prepared a letter for Allmand's signature which said the matter was some kind of mistake and, "I have been assured by the RCMP that it is not their practice to intercept the private mail of anyone." Allmand signed it and sent it off to Lawrence.

A member of Parliament had been deceived. Allmand says it wasn't his fault. The Mounties had deceived him as well. When asked about this at the McDonald Commission, Higgitt said the letter was prepared for Allmand's signature even though it was "not drafted on precise statement of fact." This was often the case, Higgitt claimed. But the minister would know the total picture. Even then, Higgitt wasn't prepared to concede that the letter was a total lie. It said mail interceptions were not a "practice" and that was true because mail interceptions, he said, weren't done every day.

There were other opportunities for the RCMP to come clean and admit that it intercepted and opened mail. In July 1975 Member of Parliament Walter Dinsdale, the Tory critic of the Post Office, read that the Federal Bureau of Investigation in the United States and other American security agencies had intercepted mail. The article left the suggestion that the FBI might have been getting information from RCMP mail interceptions. Dinsdale asked Postmaster-General Bryce Mackasey about this during the Commons question period. Mackasey began by defending RCMP and FBI cooperation in investigations of organized crime, a response that had nothing to do with the question. But he eventually got around to saying, "It is not the policy of the Post Office to permit any tampering with first-class mail by the RCMP or any other agency," and that the Post Office had "an obligation to protect the privacy of private citizens." There's never been any suggestion that Mackasey ever knew that the policy and the Post Office Act were being violated by people in his department and in the RCMP. But his reply was left to stand. The RCMP, which regularly monitors Hansard to see what is being said about the force, was content to let another minister unwittingly mislead Parliament.

In June 1972 RCMP headquarters sent out a routine procedure manual updating sheet to criminal investigators with the reminder that "Postal regulations prohibit the furnishing of information respecting mail to anyone other than the senders or the addressees" and that the Post Office Act "protects mail in transit from seizure, except under the Customs Act" for mail originating abroad. But clandestine mail interceptions and openings continued.

Twelve months later there was a Post Office foul-up that almost blew the lid off the Security Service's Cathedral operations. A field unit had authorized a thirty-day Cathedral B mail interception. The Mounties sent off a blue card containing the address of the suspect to the cooperating Post Office employee so that the suspect's mail could be intercepted. As it turned out the suspect didn't get mail that was of interest to the Security Service. But somehow the blue card made its way into the mail stream and was delivered to the man. The man got his lawyer to complain to Ottawa. He also contacted his MP and a senator. Draper sent out a "Top Secret—Priority" Telex message to all field units "suspending until further notice" all Cathedral A, B and C operations "due to a current development which may have political implications.... No further operations are to be instituted until you are advised the suspension is lifted." The man was told that there was some kind of "administrative error" and the matter was dropped. The suspension of Cathedral operations was soon lifted.

Meanwhile, the force's drug investigators were starting to create some problems for the Post Office. Some cases were running the risk of exposing in court the cooperation between postal employees and the Mounties. Asst. Commissioner E.W. Willes, the director of the Criminal Investigations Branch, sent out a directive in December 1973 arising from the Post Office's concern "regarding the opening of parcels and substituting the contents...." In a heroin shipment, for example, most of the heroin was removed and replaced with milk sugar. Willes wrote, "The Postal Department does not wish to jeopardize the cooperation which presently exists between their investigators and our members nor restrict our drug investigations in any way. However, when it is anticipated during an investigation that the Post Office cooperation will be brought out in court proceedings the following policy is to be adhered to: Parcels or letters committed to the mail service will not be opened nor the contents interfered with...." In other words, obey the law if it looks like you might get caught.

A postal official tried again to see if there was some legal way to use the Narcotics Control Act to search for and seize drug shipments in the mail. H.I. Bloom, the Post Office's chief of investigations, asked for an opinion from J.P. Cloutier, the Post Office's director of legal services. Cloutier went through all the law books, but concluded that there was no legislation amending the Post Office Act's prohibitions against "the demand, seizure or detention of mail while such mail is in the course of post."

A few days later postal inspectors across Canada were advised that the law was unchanged. The memo, from Paul Boisvert, the Post Office's head of security and investigations, said in effect that RCMP headquarters agreed that the Mounties would try to avoid implicating the Post Office operational staff in the legally risky business of opening mail to hunt for drugs. If a case looked like it was heading to a public trial there would be liaison between the Mounties and postal inspectors. There was no flat order to refuse to cooperate.

Boisvert, a former Mountie and a municipal policeman before he joined the Post Office, told the McDonald Commission that his inspectors felt they had to maintain good, close contacts with the RCMP because the Post Office relied heavily on the force. Postal inspectors didn't have the arrest powers of peace officers and they needed the RCMP to make arrests. The RCMP also helped dispose of the explosives the Post Office found in the mail from time to time.

In 1976 the Post Office again almost blew the cover on Security Service mail tamperings with a clumsy mistake. A Hamilton man received a damaged letter that had been taped back together. The man complained to the Post Office that it looked like it had been opened by someone. The Post Office investigated and discovered that the letter was damaged by a sorting machine. In the process of investigating, however, it was learned that the man was indeed the target of Security Service Cathedral operations—a Cathedral B intercept and envelope cover photocopying. Boisvert had to make a secret report to the postmaster-general explaining that the Hamilton man's mail had been intercepted and sent to Toronto for the Security Service. Boisvert reported that this was an "isolated incident that was improperly handled by a postal inspector who is due to retire next month." His report said the RCMP gave assurances that the mail wasn't opened. It was an unfortunate lapse, but "in this instance was justified in view of the national and international implications." He concluded: "Let me assure you that I am initiating action with a view to precluding such incidents in the future." That ended the matter.

But when Boisvert testified at the McDonald Commission it was revealed that the only thing "isolated" about the incident was that the postal inspector had never forwarded the intercepted mail to Toronto before. Other photocopying was performed on Post Office premises where the mail was intercepted. Boisvert, however, said he never learned until much later that the RCMP sometimes opened the mail.

Boisvert met with senior officials of the Security Service to try to sort out the situation. He said the Mounties never used the code word Cathedral in his presence and they never told him the mail was sometimes opened. Boisvert had told them that the removal of letters from the mail stream couldn't be allowed. But in national security cases the Post Office could give some limited help for mail cover checks. It had to be cleared through Boisvert's office and the Post Office had to keep control of the mail at all times. After the meeting Boisvert sent a memo to his inspectors telling them that under no circumstances would mail be "illegally opened, delayed, tampered with or be removed from our premises. Any requests from the RCMP field units for assistance is not to be adhered to." If there was a case that seemed to be "in the best interest of Canada and the public" Ottawa would decide what assistance could be given.

The Security Service instructed its men that procedures were being tightened because Boisvert felt "as we do [that] the most stringent security possible must be afforded Cathedral at all times." The directive, signed by Asst. Commissioner Murray Sexsmith, said that all Cathedral operations were to be cleared first through Security Service headquarters. It didn't differentiate between mail cover checks and Cathedral C openings. The request for help with the supporting rationale would be provided to Boisvert "in general terms" and if Boisvert agreed he would advise his postal inspectors of "the degree of cooperation to be afforded." The memo wasn't as blunt as Boisvert's to his men about the illegality of mail tampering. But in fact there were no more Cathedral C operations approved by headquarters from then on. The men in Toronto who later opened mail in the Omura case did so on their own initiative. Headquarters, however, waited for another year before explicitly telling the field units that mail opening was illegal and that requests for Cathedral C wouldn't even be considered.

Sexsmith, who was the Security Service's deputy director-general for operations, told the McDonald Commission that he stopped mail openings because "it seemed unfair to have our people stick their necks out" and get caught breaking the law. The Mounties "could already see the storm clouds on the horizon" with the exposure of illegal FBI activities in the U.S. "We were aware that the media were convinced that there was a Watergate in Canada ... and they were desperately looking for it." Some former Mounties were beginning to talk about their activities and the risk of exposure was increasing. Nowhere in his explanation to the commission did Sexsmith say that he stopped Cathedral C simply because he thought policemen should obey the law.

Howard Draper, Sexsmith's predecessor, testified that Post Office employees were asked to cooperate "out of the goodness of their hearts" as loyal Canadians. Such "collaborators ... were the most valuable asset" to the Security Service. They were never paid for their help.

In September 1977 — three months after the McDonald Commission was created and when other Mountie illegalities started to surface — the Security Service for the first time sought a legal opinion on Cathedral operations. Superintendent Cain of the legal branch confirmed that, "It is illegal for anyone to open and examine mail, with or without the cooperation of postal authorities, at any time after posting and before delivery." However, Cain said that he and Richard King, the Post Office's legal adviser, felt mail covers could be seen and photographed while "en route" as long as the mail wasn't detained. But there couldn't be any X-raying. (There wasn't any mention of another method for reading mail without opening it. High-intensity light projection can produce an image of the writing on sheets of paper sealed in some envelopes.)

The Security Service brass was slow to respond to Cain's legal opinion. It took three days to send out a top secret Telex quoting the advice and advising that Cathedral C requests wouldn't be considered. The CBC exposed Cathedral operations on November 8. Two weeks later Security Service headquarters felt another stern warning had to be issued. It said that postal authorities would agree to Cathedral B requests only if the photographing or photocopying was done on Post Office premises. "Under no circumstances is mail to be removed ... nor is it to be delayed for any reason whatsoever, regardless of the rationalization. It will be the duty of every area commander to ensure that this policy is strictly adhered to." This harsh notice was prompted by the discovery that Draper's 1973 instructions to get prior headquarters approval for mail openings had been ignored. Four such incidents were reported to the commission and the RCMP couldn't give any assurances that there weren't more.

The McDonald Commission tried valiantly to determine how many times mail was opened over the years. There was little way of knowing for sure. The Security Service didn't keep central records until 1970. It was known that approvals for illegal Cathedral C operations numbered about sixty. But each approval for the opening of the mail of one person might have involved many, many more individual pieces of mail. The effort to get figures from the Criminal Investigations Branch met with resistance. Thomas Venner of the CIB said this was because the force was "embarking on a unique experience" in asking "policemen to admit, in some instances, to the commission of indictable offences.... They know the probability of conviction is almost nil unless they speak up ... [and] we provide no immunity from prosecution or discipline." There was no central record such as the one Security Service kept. Most openings involved drug investigations and there were thousands of Mounties who worked on drug cases over the years. Venner said that field units were asked to try to get some figures and not to go after any specific details. "I'll never be satisfied we'll get an accurate picture," Venner said. For what it was worth, he went on, there were 699 reported cases of mail opening, many of which may have been legal customs inspections; there were also 592 reported cases of mail cover checks and 258 controlled deliveries of mail. Vancouver was the division reporting most of the activity.

Boisvert was asked to attempt to establish a figure from the Post Office's side of it. It was a hopeless task because he didn't know who had or had not cooperated with the RCMP. The Mounties, always protective of their sources, wouldn't tell him. But Boisvert had a good idea where to start. He began with his inspectors and former inspectors. Five former inspectors refused to give statements. One inspector still with the Post Office wouldn't talk because he might face disciplinary action. McDonald Commissioner Guy Gilbert asked why postmasters weren't surveyed to see what they knew or might be able to say about possible involvement of postal inspectors. Boisvert said that Deputy Postmaster-General J.C. Corkery and possibly Postmaster-General Blais—he wasn't sure about Blais—said he shouldn't interview line managers. "I'm inclined to call your internal investigation a sketchy job," Gilbert said.

The month before the CBC exposed Operation Cathedral Boisvert was told by the RCMP that mail might have been opened by the force. But Boisvert didn't tell Blais at that time. He began an internal investigation only the day after the CBC broke the story. The CBC's Joe MacAnthony, an affable Irishman, had cultivated most of his Mountie sources on this story over drinks in bars. He was as careful as the Security Service in protecting the identity of his sources. The lists of the names of the Mounties he had contacted included the names of men who were totally uncooperative. That way if the lists were found it couldn't be determined who did or didn't talk. The man who provided the Cathedral information insisted that he meet MacAnthony in an open area because he feared that the conversation could be bugged.

The story was presented on the national news on November 8, 1977, by reporter Brian Stewart. Operation Cathedral was the lead-off question the next day in the Commons question period. It was an embarrassing scene for the government when it became obvious that Postmaster-General Blais and Solicitor-General Francis Fox hadn't gotten together on the story. Blais started by telling Tory leader Joe Clark that the Post Office only gave information from mail covers. "At no time is the mail taken from the custody of the Post Office or diverted from the ordinary mail channels." Clark spotted the use of the present tense. What happened in the past, he asked. "Can he [Blais] give us the unequivocal assurance now that there have been no instances of intervention with the mail of a private citizen in any way other than that authorized by law?" Blais said, "I stand by my statement." But Clark wasn't going to let up. Blais acknowledged that policy had been "stretched"—but only once. This was the Hamilton case.

Tory critic Walter Dinsdale asked whether mail could be tampered with without the postmaster-general's knowledge. Blais said his people couldn't be involved as the CBC had alleged. It was a different story when Francis Fox got up. Fox said he had learned two months earlier that there had been mail cover checks, but he had learned only that morning that mail was actually opened.

Questions continued for several days in the Commons. Blais was reduced to pleading at one point that he couldn't determine what was going on in his own department until the RCMP gave him some information. "I'm not responsible for the RCMP," he said. (A few months later, he was. He replaced Francis Fox as solicitor-general when Fox resigned.)

Tommy Douglas of the NDP reminded Fox that no more than six months earlier Fox had told the Commons that the APLQ was an "exceptional and isolated incident." McDonald Commissioner Donald Rickerd wondered about this as well during his questioning of Asst. Commissioner Sexsmith. Sexsmith said that the Security Service fully intended to tell Fox about mail openings when it completed its internal report of all operations and presented the material to the McDonald Commission. But the CBC beat them to it. Besides, Sexsmith said, Fox's "exceptional and isolated incident" statement was "technically correct." The APLQ affair was "exceptional and isolated" because, he said, it was the only one of the RCMP's questionable operations involving both a break-in and the removal of documents. "Is there a qualitative difference between being technically correct and being completely and openly candid?" Rickerd demanded. "I've never considered them in the same context," Sexsmith answered.

It took Blais nine days to determine and publicly acknowledge that in fact some postal employees, including management, intercepted mail and turned it over to the Mounties. After the Post Office "lost control" of it "we can assume it was opened," Blais said. There "seemed to be a tradition" of this kind of activity in some places but no senior personnel knew about it, he said.

The government tried to take the offensive by shifting the issue from police lawbreaking to the need to change the law to help the police. Prime Minister Pierre Trudeau told a news conference that he couldn't get terribly upset about mail openings: "If they can catch a kidnapper or a terrorist once out of every five times, that's a good average." That figure was apparently pulled out of thin air by Trudeau. The RCMP never claimed it caught a kidnapper or terrorist one out of five times in its mail tamperings. And its only terrorist example, the Omura case, was later discredited.

Nonetheless, the government hastily introduced amendments to the Post Office Act to legalize mail openings by police. It was an affront to the McDonald Commission that the government did not wait for its recommendations. Guy Gilbert allowed himself to wonder aloud if it might not be like performing surgery before waiting for the diagnosis. But McDonald maintained a stoic silence.

Civil libertarians and newspaper editorialists were up in arms. The Canadian Civil Liberties Association said the government's decision to reward the Mounties by giving them a mail-opening bill encouraged disrespect for the law. Instead, the government's first priority should be to prosecute those who violated the federal Post Office Act. *Toronto Star* columnist George Bain wrote that the government was showing contempt for Canadians and for "the notion that government should seek to inspire public respect for law."

The government's only concession to propriety was to include a time limit on the legislation. Mail-opening authority would expire after one year. That would give the government time to examine and consider the McDonald Commission's recommendations. Trudeau said at a news conference that, "If the commission reaches the opinion that it is useless to open mail in all cases and that to have such power is not necessary, that power will be withdrawn and will not be granted. I would point out to you that it would be perhaps the only country in the world where security agents don't have the right to do this." That wasn't correct. It's illegal for police and security agents to open mail in the U.S. The CIA, which was caught, was ordered in 1977 to pay mail-opening victims $1,000 in damages for each piece of illegally opened mail.

Trudeau repeated the mistake three times. He also didn't know that the 1969 Royal Commission report had recommended that the Security Service should have mail-opening authority, a recommendation his government ignored at the time. When a reporter reminded him of that fact, Trudeau said, "Well, so we are acting seven years later . . . because it is high time we act after seven years. I guess the fact is neither the police nor the government were made to realize there were illegal operations going on." Trudeau, who is rarely placed on the defensive at news conferences, was obviously flustered. His math was wrong. It was nine years after the recommendation. And he said the police didn't know about illegal operations. The police were the very people who were breaking the law.

The McDonald Commission hearings into RCMP mail-tampering operations were held in mid-December 1977 in a borrowed Ottawa courtroom. For two days the force was on the defensive with its admissions that headquarters had sanctioned illegal mail openings. But on the third day the force had its chance to grab the initiative and launch its public relations campaign to try to sell the legalization of mail openings.

The RCMP's first star witness was Chief Supt. Gustav Begalki, a career officer who had been active years ago in one of the force's rare attempts to prosecute someone under the Official Secrets Act. (The case had been thrown out of court for lack of evidence.) Begalki was in charge of the bodyguard detail for visiting heads of state during Expo 67. Ten years later he was the Security Service chief for the Ontario region. He told the commission about the threat of letter bombs. The fact that the Post Office was legally responsible for stopping explosives in the mail didn't deter the force from making its intriguing presentation.

As his first exhibit Begalki pulled out a map that looked like it might have come from a Grade 2 geography colouring book. The continents were shown in crude outline. X's marked the spots in Europe, the Middle East, Australia and the Americas where letter bombs had been found over the years. Canada was in the centre. Canada's X was marked in the vicinity of Great Slave Lake in the Northwest Territories. The map was marked as an exhibit. Begalki's second exhibit was a series of schematic drawings showing how letter bombs work. Judge McDonald was taken aback. Should the Security Service be showing people how to make letter bombs? "You don't want to encourage criminals or maniacs," McDonald said. RCMP lawyer Richard Mongeau said that the force had thought a lot about the question of publicity in preparing this presentation: "It is obvious there are some details we won't reveal." Begalki said he wasn't a technical expert on letter bombs but he didn't think the sketches provided enough detail for anyone to go out and build one. (Ironically, the RCMP objected to revealing its technical methods of opening letters. It was learned later that steam kettles were sometimes used.)

Begalki testified that twenty letter bombs, most intended for foreign embassies in Ottawa, were found and defused in late 1972 and early 1973. What did this have to do with Operation Cathedral? Judge McDonald asked if any of the intended victims refused to let the Mounties open the letter bombs? No, Begalki admitted, but went on to say that if the Security Service couldn't intercept mail, a live letter bomb would have to be delivered even when nobody was at home. The victim would come along later and open his mail. Judge McDonald reminded Begalki that under the Post Office Act explosives are treated as undeliverable mail and turned over to the Mounties for disposal.

Begalki didn't know when to quit. He came up with another ingenious scenario. Terrorist groups often have rival splinter groups, he said. The Security Service might want to monitor the mail of a member of a splinter group without his knowledge. If his rivals sent him a letter bomb the Mounties would want to intercept it without tipping their hand that they were watching the mails. The RCMP wanted to protect the lives of everyone, including terrorists. But couldn't the Post Office continue to handle explosives in the mail, Judge McDonald asked. Begalki thought that would be dangerous. This was too much for John Howard, the commission's chief counsel. Howard pointed out that the Post Office has the technical means of detecting letter bombs. Furthermore, the only case in North America of a postal employee injured by a letter bomb involved an employee who was trying to pilfer mail.

The RCMP tried a dramatic hard sell again several weeks later with the presentation of Sgt. Arnold Kay of the Ottawa area drug squad. He brought along a bag full of soccer balls containing hashish and envelopes with LSD tabs. It was a Mountie extravaganza and the commission lawyers sat back and let the RCMP lawyers do the stage managing.

In 1972, Kay said, the governor of a district jail in North Bay, Ontario, was alarmed when he noticed many of his inmates seemed to be getting high on drugs and were ripping up the jail on Friday and Saturday nights. The RCMP was called in. A source reported that the drugs were coming through the mail. Kay held up a "reconstructed envelope" and solemnly advised the commission that there were real tabs of acid behind the postage stamp. (Kay had addressed this envelope to "Mr. Prison Inmate.") Judge McDonald stopped him there and asked whether there wasn't some concern in revealing a criminal technique for smuggling LSD. RCMP lawyer Mongeau said not really, hiding tabs of LSD behind postage stamps was a fairly well known technique in the drug underworld. (It apparently wasn't that well known to the Mounties in 1972 because they opened several pieces of mail at the North Bay jail before they discovered where the LSD was hidden.) Kay said there were never any charges because inexperienced jail guards didn't keep track of who got what letters.

Kay's second example involved the Laurier Street post office in Ottawa. In 1977 the postmaster there had an undeliverable letter that had been addressed to a nonexistent post office box. Postal officials for some reason suspected the envelope contained drugs. The RCMP opened it and found tabs of LSD. The sender had dropped one number from the post office box number. The Mounties figured this out and started to monitor the mail sent to the correct box number. In all, twenty-one letters were opened. Fifteen contained LSD or heroin. The other six were letters from the overseas supplier complaining that he hadn't been paid. The case was still under investigation at the time of Kay's testimony. He didn't explain why no arrests had been made.

Next Kay produced a soccer ball with hashish stuffed inside. He showed the commission how the drug had been carefully concealed between the bladder and the outer cover of the ball and how talcum powder was used to throw the dogs used to sniff out marijuana and hash off the scent. A large burlap bag full of soccer balls had arrived in Ottawa from Pakistan, addressed to a woman who had been living in an apartment hotel, but who had since dropped from sight. Customs inspectors opened the bag and thought there was nothing in it except the soccer balls. The Mounties, however, found forty to fifty pounds of hash. Two more similar parcels arrived some months later. The woman, who was wanted on charges in the U.S., was never located.

The last case was the most recent. In late 1977 the RCMP in New Brunswick learned that a resident was going to Montreal to buy hashish. He was seen in Montreal posting a parcel back to New Brunswick. The Mounties wanted to open it, but postal officials wouldn't allow it because of the recent bad publicity about mail tamperings. The Mounties tried to arrange a controlled delivery, but word of this plan leaked out and the addressee wouldn't accept the parcel. Kay said the leak was from the Post Office.

Judge McDonald asked if the drug squad's problems could be solved if it obtained a warrant and opened the mail in the presence of the judicial officer. In large cities that wasn't usually a problem, Kay said, but even in Ottawa it was difficult to get a justice of the peace to sign warrants after eleven o'clock at night. "I guess all of Ottawa goes to bed at eleven o'clock," McDonald quipped.

While the RCMP carried the ball at the McDonald Commission hearing, Jean-Jacques Blais, the new solicitor-general, tried to sell legalized mail opening at the Justice and Legal Affairs Committee of the House of Commons. The government, Blais said, considered the bill an extension of the wiretap legislation that was to remain in force for a limited period until the commission could report. (The bill, in fact, had provisions for extension beyond one year if the government got a simple resolution in both houses, a simple task for a majority government.)

Blais suggested that the exposing of Operation Cathedral increased the risk that subversives and spies would use the mails to communicate. "We become even more vulnerable when there is public knowledge, as there is now, that there is no legal means to intercept that sort of coded message used or sent through the mail." None of the committee members pointed out to him that the Post Office Act's prohibition against intercepting mail hadn't been a big secret.

The Tories supported the bill in principle, but they wanted to hear the McDonald Commission's recommendations first. Debates raged at the committee hearings. Canadian Civil Liberties Association witnesses were castigated by Liberal backbencher Rod Blaker for not submitting their brief to each of their members for approval. Arguments arose over definitions of national security. Some MPs wanted a tougher bill, others didn't like it at all. In the process most people started to forget that the federal solicitor-general's department, which is supposed to prosecute violators of federal statutes, such as the Post Office Act, wasn't doing anything about the Mounties and the postal employees who had tampered with the mail. As the controversy died, so did the urgency of the mail-opening bill. It wasn't a major priority anymore with the government. And when the Trudeau government ran out of time and had to call an election in May 1979, the bill passed into history.

8

Taps, Bugs and Break-ins

Long before Parliament gave Canadian police the legal authority to wiretap telephones and plant bugs, the RCMP was in fact tapping phones and planting bugs. Parliament never gave Canadian police the authority to stage break-ins to plant their electronic listening devices. But the RCMP conducted break-ins to do just that. Moreover, the RCMP broke into private premises a number of times for no other reason than to snoop around. They did it when they didn't have enough evidence to get a search warrant.

When the McDonald Commission began to investigate these activities it uncovered a long history of deceit. The Mounties had told lies and half-truths to cabinet ministers, members of Parliament and to each other. When the truth caught up with them, the Mounties tried to dazzle the McDonald Commission with some fancy legal footwork without much of a leg to stand on.

In its early days telephone wiretapping was a primitive activity. The equipment was simple—a pair of alligator clips, a length of telephone cable and a headset. Attaching a tape recorder to the line was considered the ultimate in sophistication. The only skill involved was the ability to shinny up a telephone pole. Some rudimentary knowledge of the coding system for the terminals in phone junction boxes helped.

But not all of the private conversations the police might want to listen to are conducted over the telephone. Some conversations might be between two or more people in the same room. New technology solved the technical problem. Tiny microphones, easily concealed, were developed. Police discovered the bug.

Bugs, however, can't be installed from the outside as a wiretap is installed. Bugs have to be planted in the room where the monitored conversations will take place. It's often difficult to get people to let the police in to install bugs in their private homes and offices. And police don't always want people to know that a bug is in place. It's a difficult technical problem, but not insurmountable. The RCMP solved it by conducting break-ins when nobody was around, hiding their bugs and then clearing out before anyone was the wiser. They called these break-ins "surreptitious entries."

The Mounties sometimes took the opportunity provided by their surreptitious entries to kind of look around a place, peer in desk drawers and closets, check under the bed or flip through the contents of a briefcase. They sometimes brought along cameras to take pictures of what they saw. It was easy. It was often helpful for an investigation.

And then sometimes Mounties would undertake surreptitious entries with no intention of planting bugs. The sole intention was to examine and perhaps photograph the contents in private premises. These visits were conducted without search warrants. In their more serious moments the Mounties called these "intelligence probes." But among themselves the Mounties just called them fishing expeditions.

The break-ins violated all kinds of laws. But nobody worried because nobody got caught. There wasn't much concern about wiretaps either because prior to 1974 there wasn't anything in the Criminal Code to prohibit them. The Mounties forgot that the Criminal Code was only one of many laws.

There are sometimes easier ways to plant a bug than to stage a break-in. If, for example, the police know that a hotel room is to be used for a rendezvouz they can go to the hotel management ahead of time and ask for cooperation. The bug can be installed in the room before the suspects check in and can be removed when they leave. The victim of crime, such as the victim of an extortion or blackmail attempt, may also agree to the bugging of his home or office if there's a chance that the criminal is likely to make incriminating statements on the premises.

But most buggings aren't like that. The police don't have the cooperation of the owner or the manager of the premises from which they hope to gather oral evidence of wrongdoing. In these cases the surreptitious entry is the only alternative. The technical planning is fastidious. There are often preliminary break-ins to locate a likely hiding spot for the bug and to get a look at the layout of the room. Favourite hiding places for microphones are the walls and ceilings. Mounties have to drill holes for the microphones and the attached radio transmitting equipment. Paint chips have to be taken as samples so that the right colours can be matched when the bug is installed and the hole is covered over. And there may be more break-ins later to replace the battery power sources in long-term bugs. Some bugs are in operation for months.

The break-ins, of course, have to be conducted when nobody else is around. Most often there is only a limited amount of time to perform the task. Lookouts are posted. Sometimes the occupants are followed to determine whether they will be away for a five-minute walk to the milk store or for hours at a repeat showing of *Gone with the Wind* at a movie theatre.

Bugging is nerve-wracking work. Most policemen don't like it. The Mounties, however, have a specialist unit of bugging technicians. The unit is known officially as Special-I. Some jokingly call it Special Ear. The unit's expertise includes locksmithing and electronics. But in smaller centres, where the availability of Special-I technicians is limited, the Mounties will sometimes call upon private locksmiths for help.

When the Mounties plan a major, long-term bug installation they have to fill out an internal RCMP form for the signature of their officers. The preliminary technical survey form asks how the target premises are decorated, what the furniture is like, will the local police cooperate if the Mounties get caught, and what are the habits of the occupants and the neighbours. The existence of the technical survey forms and break-in methods for planting bugs were revealed in September 1977 by journalists with the

CBC program, *the fifth estate*. Some of the Mounties' bugging and wiretap artists talked with CBC's Joe MacAnthony about their work. Some excerpts:

> Mountie: There were two of us manning a wiretap and we were on the midnight shift.... We were listening to the radio. There really wasn't much activity on the phone that night, and we heard the news bulletin quoting the commissioner of the RCMP denying that the force had engaged in wiretapping. There we were, sitting there with all the equipment in front of us....
>
> Q: How many of these break and enters would you have made in a year?
>
> A: Well, it's hard to say what an average is. Sometimes I guess we've done three of four a week and another time two or three months would go by and we wouldn't do any.
>
> Q: Were they solely for planting bugs?
>
> A: Well, break-ins were usually for two purposes. One to plant a technical installation, a bugging device, or gather intelligence as it were, to look around, search for drugs in an apartment or information, look for address books, that type of thing.... You often aren't prepared for what you might find inside. The place might be occupied for one thing, which has happened, or someone might come home while you're there....
>
> Q: ...did you have an authorization to be in there at the time?
>
> A: Who can authorize a break-in? A break-in is a break-in I suppose...break-ins are common practice, and you know they're sort of standard fare, you know, an accepted way of investigating any type of crime. Probably 25 percent of them are fishing trips with no real hard evidence at that time....

Q: What's actually in the manual? What does it say about breaking and entering?

A: Well the operational manual doesn't set it out in terms of breaking and entering. It's in terms of major and minor installations. But it just goes without saying you can't install a bug without going in . . . it's just left up to you how you gain entry.

Q: When a major installation is taking place, how do you organize it? How do you lay the whole thing out?

A: It's a big investigational step and it's thoroughly discussed by the brass and there's a lot of preparatory work. You've got to go down and break into the building several times as a preliminary step. . . . I've been in several major installations and I'd say there's been anywhere from twenty to fifty men involved in one way or another.

One former Mountie interviewed by me was critical of the force's lax attitude towards electronic surveillance.

Q: The wiretap laws were changed in 1974, but what did you have to get for authorizations for wiretaps before that?

A: Nothing. Nothing. There was no control over tapping. . . . There was no control, although there should have been. We tapped phones that belonged to totally innocent people, people that had nothing to do with the case. We'd get phone numbers and we would get just one number wrong. . . . The funny thing was there was this fellow in Parliament who said we don't wiretap. I don't know who he was. The justice minister or the solicitor-general says we don't tap phones. We were tapping phones. . . .

Q: What about internal controls?

A: You mention the fact that there is current legislation

covering phones. The RCMP has never looked to legislation. The RCMP taps whatever phones it wants. There was legislation within the force. You weren't supposed to tap phones. But nobody ever knew about it. You went out and tapped the bloody phones you wanted.... And the same with bugs. You could put bugs any place you wanted....

Q: There doesn't seem to be a great public concern....

A: It's like the girl on TV who says "never mind." The Security Service is the same way. Never mind burning down barns or breaking into places. We did it.... The Canadian public for some weird reason says, "Well, if you aren't doing anything wrong you don't mind your phone being bugged." If you want your phone bugged, when you apply for a phone you should say, "I want my phone bugged." I think when you rent an apartment you should say, "I want my apartment bugged." And that should be the end of it and people who don't, don't sign the form.

There were no Criminal Code sanctions against phone wiretaps and bugs until 1974 when Parliament first required police to obtain a warrant for electronic eavesdropping operations. There were, however, other federal and provincial statutes prior to 1974 prohibiting the interception of telephone conversations. The RCMP knew about these laws at least as early as 1936, but chose to ignore them.

In 1936 Col. G.L. Jennings, the RCMP's director of Criminal Investigations, obtained a legal opinion from the Department of Justice. The government's lawyers advised that the incorporation act of 1880 for the Bell Telephone Company of Canada made it a misdemeanor to "intercept any message transmitted" on company lines. The rest of the opinion dealt with the admissibility of wiretap evidence in court. The Justice Department noted that the courts would accept such evidence even if it is obtained illegally. But exposing wiretap operations in court would tip off the underworld to the fact that the police were using this kind of investigative tool. The Justice Department recommended using taps only as an aid to locating other kinds of evidence that could be presented in court without revealing that taps were in use.

Jennings thanked the deputy minister of justice for the advice "on the admissibility of evidence obtained in an irregular manner," and passed the information along to divisional commanders "in a confidential manner." Jennings forwarded the legal opinion to commanding officers, but instead of pointing out to them that he expected the force to obey the Bell act he did just the opposite. He wrote: "It is considered that it may be necessary in connection with some of your work, more and more in the future, to resort to wiretapping.... You will note the attached memorandum mostly refers to the admissibility of evidence obtained in an irregular manner." In fact, it mostly referred to the admissibility of evidence obtained in an *illegal* manner.

Ontario had its own Telephone Act on the books for many years. But it was first used in a wiretap prosecution in 1972. Two men, one an off-duty Toronto policeman, were convicted of a Criminal Code conspiracy to violate the provincial law. The Ontario act made it an offence for a telephone eavesdropper to divulge what he heard. Judge Garth Moore, a member of the Toronto police commission, found that the two eavesdroppers tapped a union telephone with the intention of telling management what the union was up to during a strike. The decision, which was upheld in the Ontario Court of Appeal, was in effect the first wiretap conviction in Canadian history. In Ontario at least it was illegal to wiretap unless the eavesdropper was doing it for his sole listening enjoyment.

The Mounties did recognize that they had legal problems with the telephone statutes in Manitoba and Alberta. Those provinces prohibited wiretapping in clear legislation and RCMP headquarters made sure the men in the field knew about it. The ban, however, didn't apply in Edmonton where the city owned the local phone company. City bylaws didn't prohibit phone taps if the police had a judicial warrant.

Throughout the 1940s and 1950s wiretapping and bugging remained an underground activity within the force. There was no clear-cut policy from headquarters and various field units developed their own practices. Generally, a double standard developed. "Technical installations" were not encouraged on the criminal investigations side, but there seem to have been few restrictions within the Security Investigations Branch, the predecessor of the Security Service.

In 1959 William L. Higgitt, then an inspector, was the officer responsible for technical aids for the Security Investigations Branch. The Criminal Investigations Branch wanted to make use of the considerable electronic equipment that the Security Investigations Branch had available. Commissioner L.H. Nicholson agreed that CIB could use some equipment, but none for telephone tapping, Higgitt says. That was reserved for the security investigators.

A new commissioner, Charles Rivett-Carnac, was appointed in March 1959. Two months into the job he learned for the first time that the SIB was conducting break-ins to plant bugs and for intelligence probes. He suspended break-in operations. "He wasn't aware in recent years of the various advances. He said, 'Let's call a halt. Let me examine this,'" Higgitt recalls. Two months later break-ins were permitted to resume.

But internal controls were imposed by headquarters. All entries, except those for short-term installations, such as overnight bugs in hotel rooms, were supposed to receive prior approval by the director of the SIB.

The CIB started to formalize its bugging program in 1936. Break-ins to plant long-term bugs had to be reported to headquarters. The following year short-term "minor installations" were added to the reporting procedure. In 1963 there were "four technical installations and four entries," Asst. Commissioner Thomas Venner of the CIB told the McDonald Commission. The electronic surveillance program escalated considerably during the next eleven years. There were 3,288 "technical installations" involving 1,072 entries. Although bugs were being used extensively in criminal cases, headquarters still had an official ban on telephone wiretaps. The ban was frequently ignored.

In 1966 the Justice Department was considering amendments to the Criminal Code to make it a criminal offence to tap telephones or engage in other forms of electronic eavesdropping. Police, however, might be given an exemption if they obtained a judicial warrant, similar to a search warrant. The CIB didn't want anyone to know that they were already heavily into electronic eavesdropping. In a policy statement that year the director of the CIB said headquarters had to give its approval before information obtained from a bug "is divulged outside the force." The statement said bugs "should primarily be for the obtension of criminal intelligence not available through usual sources, contacts, etc., and to support investigation towards prosecution. For the present, it is imperative we avoid disclosure of such methods to the public in the interest of the overall CIB Technical Aid Program."

Also in 1966 the SIB operations started to come under the scrutiny of a Royal Commission into national security methods and procedures. SIB intelligence probe break-ins were stopped. The commission wrapped up its work and reported to the government in 1969. The moratorium on intelligence probes was lifted. It might have been coincidence. But, says Higgitt, "I think we were trying to be cautious" during the time the Royal Commission was at work.

Starting in late 1965 and throughout 1966 RCMP Commissioner George McClellan lobbied the government for the Criminal Code amendments to legalize police wiretapping. On August 22, 1966, McClellan wrote Solicitor-General L.T. Pennell on the subject. He concluded his letter by saying, "I wish to reassure you at this time that this force does not practise telephone tapping in the investigation of criminal matters." On the day the letter was written that statement was probably technically correct. McClellan, however, didn't mention the SIB's wiretap activities or raise the issue of CIB entries to plant bugs.

McClellan had an earlier opportunity to raise the subject with ranking government officials. In November 1965 he sent a nine-page brief to E.A. Drieger, the deputy minister of justice, outlining the RCMP view that it needed Criminal Code amendments so it could tap phones and plant bugs without fear of breaking the law. The amendment, he argued, should be drafted in such a way that police had clear legal authority to "surreptitiously enter a premise to effect the installation of an electronic eavesdropping device." He felt that "if a peace officer was to enter a premise under certain circumstances to install an eavesdropping device, the peace officer would be contravening certain sections of the Criminal Code, making himself not only liable for criminal prosecution, but also liable in a civil action." But McClellan didn't say that that's exactly what the RCMP had been doing for many years.

The government dragged its feet on the electronic eavesdropping issue for another six years. Draft legislation wasn't introduced until 1971. The Mounties continued their wiretapping and bugging activities throughout this period.

In 1967 M.F.A. Lindsay, the new commissioner, sent another policy directive to field commanders. It said that headquarters recognized the importance of electronic "technical aids," but "it is most essential such activities not arouse public attention." In bugging operations "security is the prime requirement" and knowledge of "all technical aid operations is to be restricted to those directly involved on a 'need-to-know' basis." He reminded the units that phone tapping by criminal investigators was still prohibited. Some Mounties ignored the prohibition.

There was a slight change in policy in 1967. For the first time field units were allowed to share the fruits of their labour with other police departments and provide them with information obtained from bugs. The Mounties were developing joint investigations with other police forces, particularly in areas of organized and white-collar crime. Some of the other forces, such as the Toronto police, conducted phone wiretaps. In 1969 RCMP officers in the Toronto division wanted to know what position they were in regarding joint investigations when the Toronto police tapped phones. Asst. Commissioner J.R.R. Carrière advised "as long as city police assume responsibility for wiretapping, we, in the field of criminal intelligence, will take notice of that technique. It would be wrong for us to ignore the opportunity to obtain intelligence in this manner through cooperation with the MTPD [Metropolitan Toronto Police Department]." The Mounties could help out by transcribing tapes for the Toronto police, but they couldn't help install the tap or man the listening posts, Carrière said.

Ottawa headquarters showed periodic nervousness about the chance that the public might find out about RCMP buggings. The brass didn't want any kind of a flap while there was still hope that the government might come in with electronic eavesdropping legislation. Information from bugs was to be used as evidence in court only in investigations of "major prominence" and then only when there was no other way to get a conviction. Criminal investigators were warned to avoid compromising the Special-I technicians at all costs. Headquarters didn't want Special-I staff to have to get into a witness box where they might be subject to cross-examination. There were all kinds of dangers if a lawyer asked such questions as, "What's your job in the RCMP?" or, "How did you get inside to plant the bug?"

Carrière sent out a reminder that while presenting bugging evidence in court "may not in itself be harmful to the Technical Aid Program, it can open other avenues to defence counsel that are not in the public interest to disclose." He said that while there was a chance that the Criminal Code amendments might be introduced in 1969 "it is desired to avoid public attention to our use of these devices."

Assistant Commissioner Venner had learned about buggings and break-ins during his career with the CIB. He felt a bit personally embarrassed that he could never get lock-picking devices to work for him. But he learned something new in 1973 when he took over as chief of criminal intelligence in the Toronto division. Mounties there were conducting phone wiretaps in criminal cases in contravention of headquarters' policy. "I considered policy just that, a guideline," Venner said. He told the McDonald Commission that, "it was immediately apparent that it was virtually impossible to do investigations in Metro without taps. We would be out of business. Taps were being done to a very high degree" as an "underground activity" not reported to superiors. There were "unhealthy games" being played by Mounties who were being forced to go into court and face the choice "of admitting policy was violated or committing perjury." Venner decided to let his men continue to tap and "I took the responsibility" including the responsibility of not reporting it to Ottawa. Venner eventually told one of his superiors. The boss was "disappointed and surprised." But there was no formal reprimand and no disciplinary action.

The McDonald Commission tried to determine how high up in

the chain of command the knowledge existed that Mounties were conducting break-ins to plant bugs or carry out intelligence probes. Specifically, did solicitors-general know what was going on? The first clue was a 1968 memo retrieved from the RCMP's files by the commission's investigators. It dealt with a bugging operation in Vancouver and a briefing that was held for John Turner, then the solicitor-general. Turner served in the portfolio for only a short time and the briefing was held the day before he left to become justice minister.

The memo, written by Commissioner Lindsay, said that he, Higgitt of SIB and Asst. Commissioner H.S. Cooper of CIB met with Turner and his deputy, T.D. MacDonald, to brief the minister "very generally on the sensitive topic of our electronic intrusion in connection with crime." Turner asked about the legal implications "and we advised there was no legal bar, except a case against us for civil trespass, to which Mr. T.D. MacDonald agreed." Turner, according to the memo, was told "the difference between major and minor intrusions.... We did explain that detailed study was given each case by our experts, that great precautions are taken in each instance, and that we realize we are 'on our own' in these operations." Turner was told "so that in the event of the one miscalculation out of 500 and something going wrong, he would not be totally uninformed and surprised.... The discussion was general in nature. In conclusion the minister commented: 'Gentlemen, thank you for these very general discussions. No details of files were discussed with me.'" But what exactly was Turner told? The reference to a possible civil trespass case suggests that he was told of surreptitious entries.

In a 1978 interview Turner said he was sure he was never told that break-ins were involved. "The word was intercept.... I knew that there would be interceptions ... they didn't give details of the methods." Turner was reluctant to say more, but he acknowledged, "I wasn't likely to cross-examine them too thoroughly the day before leaving the portfolio."

T.D. MacDonald, Turner's former deputy, said in a separate interview that he couldn't remember the meeting at all. Furthermore, he didn't remember the subject of break-ins or surreptitious entries ever being raised by the Mounties during the two years he was deputy solicitor-general.

The McDonald Commission discovered other documents suggesting that in 1972 Justice Minister Otto Lang and Solicitor-General Jean-Pierre Goyer were told that planting bugs involved break-ins. The memos were written by Higgitt, by that time the commissioner, and Insp. J.V. Cain of the RCMP's legal branch. The memos describe the RCMP's meeting with the two ministers to discuss the proposed electronic eavesdropping amendments to the Criminal Code. Higgitt's memo says the force wanted to get the ministers to agree that taps and bugs should be authorized by the solicitor-general and provincial attorneys-general rather than a judge because judges might balk at the idea of surreptitious entries. Cain wrote that "the propriety of superior court judges granting an authorization, after demanding details and learning that unorthodox (perhaps illegal) methods (trespassing) might have to be committed, was raised by the commissioner." The brackets and the words "perhaps illegal" and "trespassing" are Cain's.

Higgitt told the McDonald Commission that trespassing wasn't the only legal concern he raised at the meeting. He was worried too about willful damage to a premise, stealing a key to enter a home or asking someone else to do it for the RCMP. But he was hard to pin down on whether he told the ministers these things might happen in the future or whether they had in fact happened in the past.

Goyer was given a briefing about Security Service activities in January 1971, shortly after he became solicitor-general. It included a tour of RCMP facilities. A memo by Director-General Starnes says that during the tour Goyer was shown where the wiretaps and bugs were recorded. Goyer even listened in on one for awhile.

About six months later Starnes got a memo from Robin Bourne, head of the newly created police and security planning and analysis group within the ministry. Bourne said that Goyer wanted a monthly report on the number and locations of eavesdropping operations in progress. But he added that Goyer wasn't interested in learning about "the operational side of these activities such as how various devices are installed."

Still another memo written at about the same time suggests that the Mounties withheld knowledge of break-ins to plant bugs. This was a memo from Starnes to Higgitt. Starnes wrote that in compliance with Higgitt's suggestion Goyer was not given an RCMP document that said electronic eavesdropping operations "are or may be outside the law." In explanation, Higgitt testified that "for some reason or another" he decided Goyer didn't need to see the document. "You don't go out of the way to put ministers at risk," Higgitt said.

Warren Allmand succeeded Goyer as solicitor-general in 1972. During his term he learned about intelligence probe break-ins to search homes and offices without a search warrant. But as long as the Mounties didn't take anything, he told the McDonald Commission, he thought it was legal. The Mounties told him so.

The issue of intelligence probes might have caused some trouble for the RCMP and the government during 1974 if anybody had been paying attention to the newspapers. In October of that year an article appeared in *Le Devoir*, which described Operation 300, the Security Service's general code name for break-ins. The article was based on an academic paper written by Guy Tardif, a former Mountie who was then a University of Montreal professor. (Tardif later became a provincial cabinet minister in the PQ government of René Lévesque.)

Federal ministers are briefed regularly on what newspaper stories might result in questions during the Commons question period. Allmand's aide, Georges Vincent, told Allmand about the *Le Devoir* story which touched upon "a very sensitive topic." Vincent's suggested reply for Allmand was to say only that, "I am aware of the article and am examining it."

But nobody in the Commons asked a question. The matter was forgotten soon by Allmand. Allmand told the McDonald Commission that if the opposition parties had raised the matter and had pressed him he probably would have sought a legal opinion. "But the whole thing just fell out of sight... unfortunately."

For Goyer, ignorance may have been bliss. For Allmand, the

assurances of the RCMP that their intelligence probes were legal was enough.

Supt. William Wylie of Special-I said that when the Criminal Code electronic eavesdropping amendments were introduced in 1972 the Mounties were upset because the amendments didn't include explicit authority for policemen to make surreptitious entries to plant bugs. The force raised the question with officials of the Justice Department, but the Justice Department wouldn't go for it. Without specified entry authority it remained "a question that begged for answers and we got various answers [from Justice] over several years. None were written down."

The McDonald Commission had a tough time trying to figure out how many times the RCMP went on intelligence probe fishing-trip break-ins without search warrants. The Security Service didn't start to keep records like these until 1971. The number of reported cases between 1971 and 1978 was forty-seven. These didn't include buggings. The CIB never kept records, but Venner thought he could get an answer by sending out a questionnaire asking field commanders how many times illegal entries had been made. Not surprisingly, most of the answers were zero. By rewording the question, a figure of more than four hundred was arrived at. But the lock-picking unit in Vancouver had things screwed up. Their work order records, it was later discovered, included a lot of entries for which there were legal warrants or the owners knew of the operation and had given their consent. The commission never got a straight answer.

Meanwhile, the *Globe and Mail's* sources said that the number of break-ins without warrants might run into the thousands. They were just never reported to superiors if nothing of value was found. Even many productive break-ins were never reported. One source told *Globe* reporter Lawrence Martin that the record keeping varied across the country. "You don't try to snow a guy who's done that same sort of thing. But others not experienced in that line of work were kept in the dark." Many CIB investigators laughed when they learned that the Security Service was keeping statistics on break-ins.

The Mounties hid their tap, bug and break-in activities from Parliament. The Commons Justice and Legal Affairs Committee started considering the electronic eavesdropping question in the late Sixties. Representations were made by civil liberties groups, the Canadian Bar Association and the Canadian Association of Chiefs of Police. In its 1970 report the committee said that, "law enforcement officials appearing as witnesses were extremely reluctant to furnish the committee with facts, figures and methods of operation relating to police activity in the interception of communications. Given the questionable legality of these activities and the lack of any clear public policy in relation thereto, present police wiretapping operations must necessarily be the subject of sub-rosa 'understandings' between police forces, police commissions and governmental officers. . . . " The committee saw a "patent need" for federal legislation to control police wiretapping and outlaw electronic eavesdropping by all others. Hesitating, the report went on, would only undermine public confidence in the police if there were much public exposure of wiretapping.

Wiretapping was only half the story. The committee had a second chance to learn about the bugs and break-ins sixteen months later when then Justice Minister Turner at last introduced the government's proposed Criminal Code amendments. The bill was euphemistically titled the Protection of Privacy Act. But everybody called it the wiretap bill. The bill outlawed all forms of electronic eavesdropping, except by police. Police, however, had to obtain a warrant either from a judge in criminal cases or the solicitor-general in national security cases. The bill's dry legal jargon didn't distinguish between phone wiretapping equipment and bugging devices. The committee members were able to figure out the difference, but nobody from the government or the RCMP spelled out how bugs were to be installed. Nobody ever said how bugs had been planted in the past. And nobody ever said that break-in methods were used for intelligence probes when no bugging was involved.

Committee members were shackled by rules that favoured the government. There were ten-minute time limits for questioning by each member. There were few opportunities to call RCMP witnesses. And when Mountie witnesses did show up they gave trick or evasive answers and ducked pointed questions.

Besides, there were few on the committee who were in the

mood to take a hard line with the RCMP. This was before the scandals were exposed and 1973 was the RCMP's centennial year. MPs were more interested in knowing if the Musical Ride would perform in their hometowns than in how electronic listening devices were installed. There were a few MPs, however, who came pretty close to discovering the truth.

Commissioner Higgitt appeared before the committee on May 29, 1973. Gordon Fairweather, a New Brunswick Tory and a staunch civil libertarian, asked, "Is the force wiretapping now?" Higgitt stalled: "Mr. Fairweather, we are dealing now with, I think, operational techniques. And if my minister was here, I am sure he would say that it is a little difficult for me to publicly discuss our operational techniques." Fairweather moved on to ask why the Mounties were charging admission to the Centennial Review.

Trevor Morgan, an Ontario Tory lawyer, tried to get back to wiretapping by asking if taps were used for criminal or political purposes. Chairman James Jerome, a Liberal, ruled the question out of order. Morgan persisted and Liberal backbencher Hugh Poulin jumped in. The procedural hassle ate up Morgan's allotted time for questions.

Terrance O'Connor, a Tory, tried a third time. Higgitt again stalled, pleading that Solicitor-General Allmand wasn't present. O'Connor reworded his question and unwittingly strayed into the much broader area that the force most dreaded talking about. O'Connor asked if the force employed "electronic surveillance methods?" Electronic surveillance included bugs and bugs meant break-ins. Jerome asked Higgitt if he wanted to answer the question. Higgitt thought for awhile and felt he could get out of the woods by rewording O'Connor's question. "If I could answer by recalling a question that you were about to ask me a moment earlier, putting aside security and so on, which you said you did not want to discuss, you said: does the force use wiretapping?" O'Connor fell for it. Higgitt responded, "My answer to that is no." That was official policy for the CIB and there's no indication that Higgitt knew at the time that policy was being violated.

In subsequent committee meetings Tory and NDP MPs stumbled and fumbled a bit closer to asking the right questions. They finally extracted the admission that the RCMP conducted wire-taps in security cases and "microphone intrusions" in criminal investigations. The only example given was that of police being let into hotel rooms. "I've been kicking myself that I didn't cross-examine more thoroughly," committee member Ron Atkey, a Tory, said in 1978 after the revelations at the McDonald Commission. He went on, "There was a lack of clarity. They were so close-mouthed about bugging. The question never arose in my mind that they would break in."

The wiretap bill made its way through the committee and both houses and was proclaimed law on July 1, 1974. It was a happy Dominion Day for the police. Justice Department officials held seminars and short courses across the country to explain to policemen how they could get electronic bugging and wiretap-ping warrants. It was during this period that Special-I asked the Justice Department if the Mounties could break in to plant bugs. John Scollin, a senior Justice Department lawyer, gave an oral opinion that the power to install a bug implied the power to do whatever is required to install it. But the courts would have to decide if that opinion is correct, Scollin conceded in a 1978 inter-view. Scollin suggested to the Mounties that to play it on the safe side they should include in their applications for warrants a re-quest for authorization to "install, monitor and remove" listening devices. The Mounties tried that out on some judges in British Columbia, but the judges wouldn't go for it. Scollin's opinion hasn't been tested in court, probably for a couple of reasons. The whole idea behind a surreptitious entry is not to get caught. Mounties haven't been caught in the act. In addition, not all judges might be as sharp as the B.C. judges. They might not ask whether they are granting a wiretap or a bug authorization. If they know it's a bug they might not think to ask how the bug will be planted. The applications by police and the authorizations pre-pared for the signature of the judges are bereft of these details.

Superintendent Wylie of Special-I enlightened the McDonald Commission about another piece of RCMP legal legerdemain known as "spin-off wiretaps." In the first few months of the new wiretap law members of the force used what they called the "bas-ket clause" in the court authorizations to expand the number of wiretaps they were employing in any particular investigation. It worked this way: the Mounties would investigate what they believed might be a criminal conspiracy. They knew the identity of one of the alleged conspirators. They would present their case to the judge who would authorize the interception of the private communications of the one identified person. Other people would phone this individual and because of what the police overheard they would suspect these other people might be in on the conspiracy. The police would move on to tap the phones of these other individuals without getting further authorizations. It was a neat device and the chain could go on and on. But headquarters put a stop to this practice before all the phones in Canada were tapped.

Donald Rickerd, a member of the McDonald Commission, became intrigued with the way the Mounties stretched their authority to intercept communications. He asked Venner of the CIB what the outer limits were. Venner thought that the Mounties might be able to temporarily remove someone's car to take it away and plant a bug in it. Rickerd, usually an unexcitable man, asked if this logic would "extend to all of my possessions?" Venner thought it could. "What about my desk or my chair?" Rickerd continued. Yes, Venner said, a court bugging authorization could allow the temporary removal of a desk or chair. "What if I had a guard at my premises? Could he be removed and detained to permit entry?" Venner answered that if there was no other way to get in, detaining the guard "would be defendable." His voice rising in apparent disbelief, Rickerd asked: "What if I am guarding my premises and police officers come along with an order ... could they remove me?" Venner couldn't imagine that happening because the idea of a bugging job is to catch the occupants unaware that they are being monitored. RCMP lawyer Richard Mongeau tried to rescue his client. He said that Rickerd was raising impractical and hypothetical examples. Rickerd wasn't buying. "I've seen too many instances of impractical matters being attempted" by the RCMP, he said.

When the commission turned its attention to intelligence probes, the fishing expeditions without search warrants, RCMP lawyers tried to argue that they were legal. The breaking and entering section of the Criminal Code says it's a crime to break in with the intent of committing another crime. This is usually interpreted as intent to steal something or to cause damage. Since the Mounties weren't taking anything or causing damage they thought they had no legal problems. The Mounties didn't get a written legal opinion about their theory of law until two days after the McDonald Commission was created. It wasn't very reassuring news. L.P. Landry, an assistant deputy attorney-general, wrote that entries "may have violated the provincial laws" against trespass. But there were time limits for starting prosecutions and therefore the Mounties didn't have to worry too much.

In October 1977 Superintendent Cain of the RCMP's legal branch gave a further written opinion. He noted that surreptitious entries are wrongful acts in common law and the victims can sue "irrespective of whether or not any damage to the property, or anything in it, occurred." He cautioned against members of the force saying that such entries were lawful simply because there was no criminal intent to steal something or damage property. "... we must take care not to confuse that position with the situation where conduct of our members is clearly legal and ethically proper in every conceivable respect and of which there is no valid criticism," he wrote. Cain said the lack of criminal intent argument leads logically to saying policemen can surreptitiously enter anyone's home every day for years "merely for the purpose of keeping track of him or to see what he was up to...." Cain didn't think the public would be too happy with that kind of reasoning.

The commission asked why Mounties simply didn't get legal search warrants. Venner said it wasn't always easy to convince a judge or a justice of the peace that the police have "reasonable and probable grounds" that they'll find evidence of criminal activity in a search. The police should be able to exercise their own discretion.

There are several faults with Venner's reasoning. To begin with, the Criminal Code doesn't say that there must be probable grounds. There need be only reasonable grounds. And if a judge or justice of the peace isn't convinced the police have reasonable grounds then he must think the police have unreasonable grounds. The law was intended to prevent unreasonable searches. Furthermore, the law was written to keep policemen from exercising their discretion. The discretion rests with the judge or the justice because the lawmakers wanted some independent authority to weigh the evidence to determine if there's some reasonable basis for a search.

In further testimony Venner said that civil trespass law and provincial trespass statutes weren't given a lot of consideration when the Mounties planned intelligence probes. His fall-back position was that if intelligence probes are illegal they are "defendable morally and ethically." Besides, "not everything can or should be codified or provided for in legislation [concerning] police activities.... If everything is being provided for in law then police discretion disappears ... this is not desirable for society." Judge McDonald didn't like what he was hearing. He told Venner that "officials of government are not permitted to do things that aren't permitted by law, even if it's not the criminal law." Rickerd said it's pretty frightening to think policemen were going on fishing trips "without the vaguest idea of what they might find." Venner said, "I suspect that has happened."

The last line of defence for the force was the argument that some judges had reviewed cases of surreptitious entries and hadn't found anything improper. Wylie of Special-I had a transcript of such a case with him. Judge McDonald was sceptical. He read the transcript and discovered that that wasn't the situation at all. The trial judge had permitted the introduction of the evidence obtained through an entry, but was silent on how the evidence was obtained. Canadian courts have long allowed illegally obtained evidence to be entered.

Wylie said that the RCMP was disappointed that Parliament "failed to address" the question of whether a bugging authorization carried with it the authority to enter surreptitiously in order to plant the bug. He later said Parliament had adopted the force's view that it did. Rickerd picked up this apparent inconsistency. With remarkable candor, Wylie said, "These are opinion statements of ours and are not presented as fact or even close to fact."

The Security Service was pretty closemouthed about its break-in operations. Details were discussed in in camera hearings because of national security. But Asst. Commissioner Stanley Chisholm told a public hearing that the practice dated back to at least the late 1950s. The Security Service broke in to hunt for things like secret code books. The Security Service was vague about its legal justification. The Official Secrets Act, however, allows RCMP officers with the rank of superintendent or higher to authorize "in case of great emergency" a search and seizure of "any sketch, plan, model, article, note or document, or anything" that might be evidence of a violation of the act. Otherwise, they have to get a search warrant from a justice of the peace. The act seemed to contemplate situations like a spy being stopped in the process of transmitting official secrets by radio. It's hard to imagine any "great emergency" in intelligence probe operations when meticulous plans for entry are made days or weeks in advance.

The 1974 amendments to the Criminal Code were a belated attempt to try to impose some control over invasions of privacy that were already completely out of control. The law recognizes that there may be times when a person's privacy has to be invaded in the legitimate search for evidence of criminal wrongdoing. With search warrants the invasion of privacy is recognized as it occurs and the individual has recourse to the courts if he feels he has been the innocent victim of a police mistake. Wiretaps and bugs, with or without court authorization, are a more insidious privacy invasion because it may be years before the individual knows what has happened. The tape recorder and microphone pick up all conversations, innocent or guilty, and can entangle the target's spouse, children or neighbours as easily as the target. Break-ins of the intelligence probe variety are beyond even the modest controls of a judicial warrant. They represent a wanton and criminal disregard for individual privacy and the RCMP carried them out because the force felt it would never get caught.

9

Loopholes

Canadians are trusting people. Most believed that the confidentiality provisions in the income tax laws would guarantee that information about their private financial affairs would go no further than the tax collector. And they believed the assurances of Prime Minister Lester Pearson and his cabinet ministers in the mid-Sixties that the new Social Insurance Numbers would never be used in a police-state kind of identity card system for keeping track of the whereabouts of people.

But then again, most Canadians didn't reckon on the RCMP's subverting principles of confidentiality in its determination to compile dossiers. And who recognized the ingenious ability of the Mounties to seek out and stretch loopholes in the laws to accomplish their ends? Not only did the Mounties do these things, but they had the compliance of the civil servants whose duty it was to keep the secrets of citizens. And the RCMP had the cooperation of cabinet ministers who didn't ask Parliament to change the rules but instead made secret agreements to give the Mounties what they wanted. The RCMP had a boss, a solicitor-general, who was too busy to find out what was going on even when he was told by another cabinet minister that the force was involved in "technical violations" of the law.

Ironically, the Canadian government has one of the toughest

laws in the world to protect its own secrets—the Official Secrets Act. But the government has been unable to keep the secrets of its citizens. Canadians regularly entrust various government agencies with the most intimate details of their private lives. Tax collectors learn things people wouldn't tell a priest in a confessional—how much money they make, whether they've been fired, what charities they support, how much they may contribute to a particular political party, who they are paying alimony to and how much, what their medical bills are, how much they lost on bad investments and so on. A lot of this same kind of personal information makes its way into the files of the Canada Employment and Immigration Commission, the new name for the Unemployment Insurance Commission. Canadians have little choice but to tell. The same laws that are supposed to guarantee confidentiality also require citizens to disclose personal information so that they'll pay their fair share of taxes and will be able to collect from the Canada Pension Plan when they retire or the unemployment insurance program if they're out of work.

There were two general concerns when the government first started to collect income taxes in 1917 to pay for the Great War. The most obvious concern was that people don't like to pay taxes. The second was that to make it work the government had to ask Canadians to surrender a bit of their privacy. To get people to voluntarily declare their income, Parliament included confidentiality provisions in the first Income Tax Act. The confidentiality provisions are still there on paper. Canadian tax collectors for years prided themselves on being tight-lipped with confidential information. The McDonald Commission learned of the case of a Saskatchewan man who made money from illegal gambling. He didn't feel too guilty about the way he earned his money, but he felt compelled to walk into the tax office and pay his taxes. He apparently trusted tax officials not to tell the police. The basis for that kind of trust started to erode when the RCMP began to covet the information that the tax collectors were getting.

Over the years the RCMP developed a close association with the Department of National Revenue. Most of that history was secret until it was uncovered by the McDonald Commission and a provincial inquiry in Alberta.

The association started innocently enough. As policemen, the Mounties had legal powers that the tax collectors lacked. Consequently the tax officials had to call on the federal police to execute search warrants or to arrest people who were wanted on tax evasion charges. The Mounties weren't yet involved in tax investigations. But they were the muscle. As the force developed a greater scientific crime detection capability, it was natural for tax officials to take advantage of it. The RCMP crime lab, for example, was asked occasionally to test to see if charitable donation receipts might be forged.

Documents filed with the McDonald Commission show that in 1937 tax officials felt that they couldn't turn over tax records to police or anyone else even after records had been subpoenaed for use as evidence in criminal or civil court proceedings. By the mid-Sixties amendments to the Income Tax Act and various judicial interpretations had slightly altered this strict confidentiality. Tax records were still off limits for civil trials. But the records could be used in criminal cases. The confidential information, however, couldn't be divulged to police until after a criminal charge was laid. That still restricted the use of tax records until the criminal investigation was pretty well completed by the police.

As a wartime measure in 1940 the federal cabinet granted the RCMP the authority to see tax files in security cases completely unrelated to enforcement of the Income Tax Act. Cabinet rescinded the order in 1946. But the McDonald Commission found that the arrangements for providing confidential tax information continued until at least the fall of 1977, several months after the creation of the commission. It wasn't until 1978 that Security Service headquarters issued explicit orders that its members shouldn't try to contact income tax department employees in attempts to get tax data. The order also said that all inquiries normally channelled through headquarters would no longer be considered.

During the 1960s the RCMP's criminal investigators stepped up their investigations of suspected organized crime figures. To their credit, the force recognized the threat of mob operations in Canada long before many other police forces. The Mounties took their lessons from the experience of U.S. enforcement agencies.

U.S. tax investigators, Justice Department officials and the FBI worked hand-in-hand in strike force operations against mobsters during the 1960s. If the U.S. government couldn't stop the flow of illegal income it was at least determined to catch the crooks who didn't pay their taxes. It was effective.

In 1967 the RCMP wanted to try the same approach. M.J. Bradshaw and R.S. McGee of the Department of National Revenue's (DNR) special investigations division were invited over to the RCMP headquarters for a little chat with members of the National Crime Intelligence Unit. The Mounties pulled out some files on prominent organized crime figures and showed Bradshaw and McGee how much profit there was in illicit drug, gambling and other rackets. The tax men were impressed. But they were basically tax collectors. They knew from past experience that criminal investigations weren't noted for the amount of tax revenue produced. They agreed to sound out their superiors and perhaps get approval at the deputy ministerial level for cooperative arrangements. The Mounties said that approval would have to recognize that the joint investigations would be primarily for criminal prosecutions rather than tax cases. The idea was premature and nothing much came of it.

Two years later Deputy Commissioner William Kelly wrote to the deputy minister of the DNR in an attempt to revive the plan. Kelly noted that the DNR had received information from the RCMP about the activities of two underworld figures. There was nothing improper in the RCMP doing so. None of its information was covered by confidentiality provisions, such as those in the Income Tax Act, and the DNR could use such information the same way it used tips from any other source. But Kelly wanted a "two-way" exchange. Another series of meetings was held and a philosophy developed at the DNR that information could be provided to the RCMP if the Mounties were trying to help with tax collection. The information exchange was to be strictly controlled at the headquarters level of both agencies. (Official documents of the time acknowledge that "sub-rosa arrangements" already existed at the local level.) Inspector Cain of the RCMP's legal branch provided a written legal opinion that there could be disclosure of tax information to the force if its investigations would produce some tax revenue.

Senator George McIlraith, who was solicitor-general from 1968 to 1970, said the Mounties repeatedly pressured him in an effort to get access to confidential income tax files. The force wanted their minister to lobby on their behalf to get an information-sharing agreement with the Department of National Revenue. McIlraith told the McDonald Commission that he refused the requests. He told the force that they would have to get an opinion from the Justice Department on whether such an agreement would be legal. (Apparently this wasn't done.)

The Mounties also wanted McIlraith to check with the DNR to see if the tax collectors were following up on tips provided by the force about suspected organized crime figures. "I told them it was none of their business," McIlraith told the commission.

The RCMP didn't waste much time in renewing its pressure to get easy access to confidential files when Jean-Pierre Goyer became solicitor-general. John Starnes of the Security Service wrote Goyer in June 1971 explaining the Mounties' perceived need for both unemployment insurance and tax data. "I recognize that there would be political and other difficulties in the way of seeking to amend legislation merely to meet the needs of the Security Service," Starnes wrote. But "we believe that with ministerial agreement arrangements could be worked out with the different departments and agencies concerned to meet our requirements within the framework of existing laws and in a manner which would attract no attention or criticism."

Goyer seems to have been more cooperative than McIlraith. A month later he wrote to Revenue Minister Herbert Gray and Labour Minister Bryce Mackasey, the minister responsible for the Unemployment Insurance Commission. Goyer asked his colleagues to agree to discussion by departmental officials on whether the Security Service could be given permission to see files "in a manner which would attract no attention or criticism."

W.L. Higgitt, the RCMP commissioner at that time, thinks Goyer's efforts helped loosen up things with the tax department. Higgitt told the McDonald Commission that the force had been "only partially successful" with the tax department until 1971.

The Income Tax Act is rather vague on the point of who in the government can have access to tax records. It says "officials" and "authorized persons" may divulge information to other authorities who are assisting in tax collection. It was a loophole the Mounties exploited to the fullest. The RCMP didn't want to collect taxes so much as it wanted access to the tax files of organized crime suspects. If the Income Tax Act could be used for subsequent prosecutions, so much the better. But the force would be more than pleased with prosecutions under the Criminal Code alone.

On May 25, 1972, the cabinet agreed that the tax collectors and the police should be working together. The government had two possible choices. It could announce its intentions and bring in amendments to clear up the ambiguity of the Income Tax Act or it could agree with the RCMP interpretation of the loophole in the act. The government decided to do the latter and approved a "memorandum of understanding" between the DNR and the RCMP. Furthermore, the government decided to keep the agreement secret. The elaborate secrecy which surrounded the document for more than five years suggests that officials at the highest levels of government had misgivings about the propriety of what they were doing.

The memorandum says clearly that the intention is to "cause maximum disruption of organized crime." Only incidentally is prosecution under the Income Tax Act mentioned. It says that the minister of national revenue "hereby designates the members of the Directorate of Criminal Investigations" of the RCMP as "authorized persons" able to receive confidential income tax information. There were two problems with that provision. The Income Tax Act doesn't permit the minister to designate anybody as anything. Either they are or they aren't "authorized persons" under the act and that is a question open to interpretation. The second fault was potentially more serious. The RCMP initially wanted twenty-two members of the force designated as recipients of confidential information. But the wording would include almost every single member of the force except those in the Security Service. There were thousands of "members of the Directorate of Criminal Investigations" performing duties ranging from snowmobile patrol in the Yukon to the issuing of parking tickets at Toronto International Airport. Given the Mountie's ability to increase the circumference of loopholes, the agreement could be (and was) used to pass along tax information to investigators who had nothing to do with the organized crime project, much less income tax collections. It was open season on the tax files.

The agreement turned policemen into income tax collectors and to a much greater extent turned tax collectors into policemen. The RCMP designated twenty-two members of the National Criminal Intelligence Unit and the commercial fraud squad as the force's liaison with the DNR. The tax department still had reservations and fears that disclosure of the agreement would undermine voluntary tax reporting. Tax officials were promised that information from tax files wouldn't be disseminated outside of the force and would be kept within the strict "need-to-know" confines of the RCMP. The promises were later broken.

The RCMP used its extensive criminal intelligence files to come up with the names of almost a thousand people who were suspected of organized crime activity. These "targets" had their tax returns audited and their financial affairs closely scrutinized by both the RCMP and DNR. In four and a half years, the Department of National Revenue was able to make tax assessments against the targets of about $15 million. There were 591 convictions for tax-related cases and fines of more than $300,000 were levied. Despite the initial misgivings of the tax department, the program proved to be a revenue-generating activity beyond all expectations.

In addition to the legal problems of information sharing, the joint program raised a number of other ethical issues that the agencies never resolved, if indeed they were ever considered. What, for example, was the morality of a government knowingly living off the avails of criminal activity? The intention of the agreement was to fight organized crime by attacking its wealth. But in many cases the government was settling for its share of the profits. The moral dilemma could only be resolved if the force of criminal law could be used as an additional sanction against the crooks. The available evidence in many instances couldn't sustain a criminal prosecution but could be used successfully in tax cases. The RCMP and DNR were in the position of saying, in effect, "We know that you aren't earning your wealth honestly, but we can't prove that you are guilty of a specific crime. So we're just going to have to tax you to the limit." To many crooks, the money involved was so substantial that they were more than willing to give Ottawa its cut.

The second problem appears to have gone unrecognized by the tax department. The Mounties had their foot in the door with access to tax files. There were some members of the force who didn't understand or who deliberately ignored the restrictions that were supposed to control dissemination of tax information. Sgt. Victor Pobran, for example, told the McDonald Commission that he saw nothing wrong if, as a last resort in a major case, biographical information from tax returns was passed on to other Mounties. Pobran was one of the seventy-five commercial crime section investigators who were eventually named as "authorized" recipients of tax data. He thought he could use his access to help other investigators get "biographical" information including the names of the charities and political parties to which a person contributed.

Sgt. Tony Kozij of Winnipeg told the commission that he thought all RCMP investigators other than those in the Security Service could get tax information. The Winnipeg commercial crime section passed along information to the drug squad. The information from tax returns included the name of a person's previous employer, his income, the location of his rental property, the income from the property and income data about the person's spouse and dependents. The Winnipeg RCMP customs and excise section got the names of a company's employees, accountants, rental properties and shareholders. In all there were fifty-one cases in Winnipeg in which tax data got beyond the commercial crime section, including one disclosure to another police force. The same sort of thing was happening in Ontario, New Brunswick and Nova Scotia.

In one case in Truro, Nova Scotia, a man had his tax files examined and the information passed along to an RCMP drug squad merely because, according to a Mountie memo, he "appeared to be living beyond his means and flashing a lot of cash around. . . ." The man had just recently arrived from Ontario. The Mounties thought he must be some kind of drug dealer to have all that cash. The tax information, however, showed that the man "was financially secure" and he was cleared of suspicion. The incident may say something about the suspicious minds of policemen or the state of the economy in Truro.

Naming a person as a "target" because of suspected organized crime activity also raises questions about civil liberties. This is because the RCMP's working definition of organized crime is so broad and vague. The force says, "organized crime means two or more persons concerting together on a continuing basis to participate in illegal activities either directly or indirectly for gain." Insp. R.D. Crerar, the head of the commercial crime branch at headquarters, conceded to McDonald Commission lawyer John Sopinka that the definition in its broadest use could include a husband and wife who are cheating on unemployment insurance claims. Crerar said, however, that the RCMP would use common sense before designating a person a target. That prompted Judge McDonald to paraphrase *Alice in Wonderland*—"I know what organized crime is. It's what I say it is."

It was when the RCMP and DNR tried to stretch the terms of the secret 1972 agreement that both agencies got into trouble. In 1975 the Mounties were investigating an alleged kickback and bribery scheme involving an American carnival company which operated at the annual Edmonton Exhibition. The Department of National Revenue got involved in a police seizure of the company's books. The investigation reached the point where an Exhibition official was charged with accepting a bribe. When officials of the provincial attorney-general's office were preparing the case for trial, they discovered what they believed were improprieties in the way the seized documents were obtained and shifted around between Edmonton city police and DNR officials while the carnival company tried a legal manoeuvre to quash the original search warrant. Alberta Attorney-General James Foster ordered the bribery charges dropped because of "tainted" evidence. Foster also ordered a provincial inquiry under Alberta Supreme Court Justice James Laycraft to determine what funny business the DNR and RCMP had been engaged in. Foster was Alberta's chief law officer and was directly responsible for the administration of justice in the province. But he was never told of the secret agreement between the DNR and RCMP. In fact, Edmund Swartzack, the tax official involved in the case, had seized the documents from the Edmonton city police to keep details of the agreement secret. Swartzack told Laycraft he'd acted upon the orders of his superiors in Ottawa in the hope that he would avoid a subpoena to testify about the original search and seizure. He said, "It became evident that if I were then subpoenaed to testify, the extent of our participation would become known ... that had to be avoided at all costs since the minister had made no announcement to date with respect to our mutual cooperation."

The Laycraft inquiry forced the government to reveal the existence of the secret agreement and the text of the 1972 memorandum of understanding. In releasing the text in 1977, Solicitor-General Francis Fox and Revenue Minister Joseph Guay said there was nothing sinister in the fact that the arrangement had been kept secret for more than four years. In a joint press release, the ministers said, "It was decided at its inception that maximum tactical advantage would be gained only as long as the new strategy was not common knowledge." The ministers never explained what it was that suspected organized crime figures could have done to avoid detection and prosecution if the joint program were known.

The government practised such secrecy again when Sopinka of the McDonald Commission wanted to make public a 1976 exchange of correspondence between two previous ministers — former Revenue Minister Bud Cullen and former Solicitor-General Warren Allmand. Government lawyers argued that the correspondence shouldn't be released because they were "privileged cabinet documents." Reporters got a hint a few days later that there might be another reason for not disclosing the documents when Sopinka, in a passing remark, said there was a letter from a former revenue minister to a former solicitor-general suggesting that the Mounties were doing something wrong. Government lawyer Allan Lutfy immediately objected to any mention of correspondence between ministers until the question of cabinet privilege was resolved.

When the documents were finally revealed, a year later, it turned out that indeed Cullen had worries about the legalities of giving information to the Mounties. In May 1976 a Department of National Revenue employee told Cullen that the Mounties were "unofficially" getting tax information for cases other than income tax evasion investigations. Moreover, the RCMP was passing the information along to other police forces. One of Cullen's aides did some investigating and reported back that these activities went beyond anything contemplated in the secret 1972 agreement. Cullen issued orders to his department in July to stop the practice.

At about this same time the Mounties wanted to reveal the existence of the secret 1972 agreement. Warren Allmand, who was then solicitor-general, wrote to Cullen asking if there were any objections to making the agreement public. Cullen wrote back, advising that his department officials didn't like the idea. Cullen added: "... that another concern of my department in this connection lies in the fact that when tax information is provided to the force for purposes other than those of the Income Tax Act, a technical violation of the act is involved."

Allmand told the McDonald Commission that when he learned of this he didn't do anything about it. The way Cullen had mentioned "technical violations"—almost in passing—"didn't convey to me the highest priority." He didn't order the practice stopped because "I didn't know exactly what was meant" by the phrase "technical violations."

Allmand said he fully intended to get to the bottom of the "technical violations" business. "My intention was to have this thing fully aired. . . . Nobody told me it was something that had to be done in July or August. Ministers were aware of it, or at least aware there were problems even if we didn't quite know what they were." It was a busy time. The Commons was tied up with another vote on capital punishment, the Mounties were in the final stages of preparing security for the Montreal Olympics and "then the holidays after that," Allmand said. By the time fall rolled around there was a cabinet shuffle and both he and Cullen were in new portfolios.

The announcement of the agreement was put off until it couldn't be hidden any longer. Judge Laycraft in Alberta found out about it and the text was released. In his final report, Laycraft agreed with the RCMP and DNR interpretation of the Income Tax

Act that allowed Mounties to have access to tax files if they were helping to investigate tax cases. But the vindication came late in the day after years of deliberate secrecy. Laycraft's report left unresolved the issue of the use of confidential tax return information for police purposes other than income tax investigations. The disclosures at both the Laycraft inquiry and the McDonald Commission prompted the Mounties to clean up their act and strictly abide by the provisions of the agreement. The disclosures also served notice to taxpayers that they couldn't expect their government to keep confidential personal information out of the hands of the federal police. Unlike the haste with which the government moved to bring in a police mail-opening bill, the government did nothing to clarify its position or to clear up the ambiguities in the confidentiality provisions of the Income Tax Act. It could act quickly when it came to providing greater police powers, but was content to wait for the McDonald Commission recommendations before doing anything to protect and define more clearly the rights of its citizens.

The Mounties began to take an interest in the Unemployment Insurance Commission almost from its inception. As early as August 1942 the Criminal Investigations Branch started to devise methods to get around the confidentiality regulations. The regulations were strict. No information, either written or oral, obtained from an employer or employee was to be divulged outside of the UIC. There was one exception. The UIC could let other government departments and courts have unemployment insurance information. But such disclosures were only to assist with the administration and enforcement of the Unemployment Insurance Act. The UIC, for example, could call in the Mounties to help catch a UIC cheater. As with tax files, the Criminal Investigations Branch thought it could get a third exception for cases in which the Mounties were trying to track down a suspected criminal. This would be only after the suspect had been identified, charges laid and an arrest warrant issued. The UIC agreed to provide some very limited information and only in exceptional circumstances. But the Mounties had their foot in the door. By 1946 they were trying to expand their use of UIC information. A head-quarters document at that time suggests, none too subtly, that the UIC should be reminded that "the RCMP is the duly accredited and recognized federal police force and, as such, makes innumerable enquiries on behalf of the Unemployment Insurance Commission. With this in mind, it would appear reasonable to expect them to reciprocate in a far more practical manner...." This bordered on bureaucratic blackmail of the most obvious sort. The force wasn't going to bend over backwards to help UIC officials police their program unless there was some cooperation in return.

The UIC, like the Post Office and the Department of National Revenue, had only limited enforcement and investigative resources. Most of the hired hands were former Mounties who had strong loyalties to the force. Most agencies of the federal government depended on the RCMP for a great deal of assistance. The other agencies sometimes went to great lengths to keep the Mounties happy and to maintain their good will. What seems to have been forgotten was that the RCMP wasn't doing anybody any special favours. It was the force's duty to enforce other federal statutes and to assist the agencies.

Ironically, what raised the RCMP's ire with the UIC in 1946 was that the commission had asked in one particular case why the Mounties wanted information about an individual. The Mounties didn't want to tell what the suspect was wanted for, but they wanted the UIC to open up its files unquestioningly. The 1946 memo also misunderstood the point of the confidentiality regulations. In the RCMP view the regulations were to prevent disclosure only to the public. The regulations "presumably [were] not placed there for the expressed purpose of precluding access to the police, particularly to this force, to records which might disclose the whereabouts" of a suspect. If the government had wanted Mounties to have access to the UIC files the regulations probably would have said so. But the force didn't even try to determine what the government's intention was. It would have been simple enough to ask the Justice Department for a legal opinion. The risk was that the force wouldn't like the answer. Therefore the Mounties continued to bully the UIC.

By 1950 the confidentiality provisions had been changed some-what and the UIC was given discretionary powers to disclose in-formation from its files to whomever it saw fit. The Mounties moved again to expand their use of the files. The UIC agreed to provide the force with not only tracing information for criminal suspects but also tracing information for missing persons. Asst. Commissioner L.H. Nicholson assured UIC officials of discretion. The addresses of suspects would be provided to other police with-out the other forces knowing the source of the information. Miss-ing persons who had run away from home and family would be contacted by the RCMP and told of the concern of their loved ones. But a runaway's whereabouts wouldn't be conveyed to the family without his permission. S.H. McLaren, the UIC's executive director, agreed but wanted even greater discretion. In a note to Nicholson, McLaren said, "It would be appreciated if members of your force on any occasion when they are required to visit our local offices could be dressed in civilian clothing rather than in uniform."

The arrangement continued pretty well unchanged for more than a decade. As time went on it became more formalized and structured. The government took a major step in 1964 to expand social benefit programs and to introduce a nearly universal adult numbering system, the Social Insurance Numbers. The numbers that had been used previously only for unemployment insurance also became the basis for the administration of the Canada Pen-sion Plan. For the first time almost every member of the national work force would have to be numbered. There were fears ex-pressed at that time by John Diefenbaker and other MPs that the numbers would become a form of national identification card system. As mentioned previously, Prime Minister Lester Pearson and other ministers assured the Commons that this wouldn't happen.

Behind the scenes the RCMP was also giving assurances to the government that the force had no intention of trying to use the social insurance registration plan as an investigative or tracing tool. In a June 11, 1964, secret memo to all field commanders, Deputy Commissioner J.R. Lemieux wrote: "The Minister of Jus-tice has been assured by the Commissioner that, subject always to the requirements of the government, we have no intention of seeking access to this confidential data. In line with this policy no attempts are to be made by any members of the force to obtain access to this material." It wasn't that the Mounties didn't recognize the value of the information, but Lemieux told the field commanders that the question "may become an issue in the House of Commons and elsewhere and could result in unfavourable publicity for the force."

Two weeks later headquarters' true intentions became clearer. In another memo to field commanders, Lemieux said the force was to continue liaison with UIC regional offices. The new SIN central index wasn't to be integrated with UIC records for another four years. Until the integration was completed requests for information were to be directed to regional offices "as this is a most valuable source of information to investigators," Lemieux wrote.

By 1969 the RCMP had gained access to the SIN central index in direct contravention of the assurances given to the Justice Minister in 1964. For awhile requests for identification verification were channelled through A Division, the Ottawa area field unit across town from headquarters. Since the officers at A Division didn't like this extra workload, arrangements were made for all field units to Telex their requests directly to the central index. The only qualification that the UIC put on this procedure was a requirement that the RCMP's field units had to specify that the information was needed for criminal investigations.

The McDonald Commission was unable to determine whether either the UIC or RCMP ever advised the Justice Department or senior government officials or ministers that the assurances given in 1964 were no longer valid in 1969.

The RCMP found that one of the most effective ways of tracing people was through their Social Insurance Number. The SIN, according to Asst. Commissioner Henry Jensen, has become a national identity number because it is used by banking and credit institutions and a wide variety of other government and private agencies as a standard form of identification. Minor hockey leagues use SIN for computerized record keeping. Travel agencies ask for a SIN before booking charter airline flights. Cable TV companies use SIN to keep track of customers. School boards, large employers and department stores use SIN. This wasn't supposed to happen. The numbers were to be used only for administering federal social benefits. Nor were the Mounties supposed to use SIN records to keep track of people. But they did do this up until the summer of 1978 when the imminent public disclosure of the practice forced the government to cut the Mounties off from this source of information.

During the early Seventies the kind of information the force was receiving from the SIN central index was limited to identification verification of a number. Regional UIC offices, however, continued to provide information about the employment and work history of social insurance registrants. On two occasions the public was falsely told that UIC information was so confidential that even the police didn't have access to it. On January 19, 1972, the Canadian Press wire service carried a story from Ottawa quoting an unnamed UIC spokesman as saying that Social Insurance Numbers and employment information isn't released to the police. The spokesman was commenting on the complaint by London, Ontario, city police that they couldn't get UIC information for fraud investigations. The spokesman said it was longstanding UIC policy not to release information. "If we start handing this information out, people will stop getting their Social Insurance Numbers," the spokesman said. In a March 10, 1973, feature article in *Weekend* magazine, Raymond Thibault, the head of UIC's central index, was quoted as saying: "Our function isn't to provide anyone —and that includes the police—with information about our clients.... If people got the idea we were a kind of benevolent private-eye agency, we wouldn't get the correct facts we need to run the system." During that same period there were behind-the-scenes negotiations between the RCMP and the UIC. The Mounties tried to get even more information and the UIC tried to put some limits on accessibility. The RCMP lost the bureaucratic battle and access was confined to cases of "serious crime and major fraud." The crimes were specified as murder, attempted murder, armed robbery, robbery with violence, rape, attempted rape, kidnapping, aircraft hijacking and "some other acts which give rise to a good deal of public indignation." The

RCMP tried to keep its options open, but UIC officials reserved the right to spot-check RCMP case files to make sure that only major crimes were involved.

With time RCMP access to the files became routine. Requests for information were processed, sometimes within a matter of minutes, by two secretaries—one from the RCMP and one from the UIC. The RCMP kept records of the number of requests from 1974 to 1978. During that period the Mounties sought and obtained information about more than 1,600 individuals. Tony Kelly, a lawyer for the McDonald Commission, examined many of those records and couldn't determine whether they all fitted into the RCMP's definition of serious crime cases. Most of the records didn't contain any reason for the request. The McDonald Commission also discovered that the Mounties were passing along all kinds of requests from other police forces. These included police in Winnipeg, Thunder Bay, Sudbury, Medicine Hat, Kingston, Burlington and Dunes Park, Indiana. The commission found no evidence that the other forces were aware of how the Mounties got the information. The RCMP also gave confidential data to customs and excise officers, immigration officers, passport officers and foreign immigration officers.

In the course of investigating the RCMP, the McDonald Commission discovered confidential UIC documents showing that the agency had devised a plan in the early 1970s to issue every newborn baby in Canada with a Social Insurance Number. The plan received considerable support from provincial registrars of vital statistics. But it was fraught with political dangers. A 1971 UIC document says that a decision to "extend the concept to registering children from birth should only be taken in the light of at least some study of the release of information question. For example, perhaps the only way that the government would find it acceptable to register children would be on the basis of giving complete assurance to all concerned, including the public, that the most rigid attitude will be taken in this regard, perhaps even far more strict than is now the case." The plan was implemented in only one province—Prince Edward Island. The PEI registrar of vital statistics applies for a Social Insurance Number on behalf of every newborn. The PEI baby registration program had been in operation for more than five years before cabinet got around to enacting regulations in 1976 specifically permitting provincial registrars to apply for numbers on behalf of babies.

There was in important change in the Unemployment Insurance Act in 1977. The new legislation no longer left the Unemployment Insurance Commission (renamed the Canada Employment and Immigration Commission) with the discretion to release information. That discretion could only be exercised by the employment minister. The new minister, Bud Cullen, cut off the information flow in June 1978—about one week before the McDonald Commission began hearings on the issue. Cullen stopped the practice because of a belated Justice Department legal opinion questioning the legislative authority for the release of information. Cullen said that if the McDonald Commission agreed with Justice's legal opinion the government would bring in amending legislation to resume the information flow to the RCMP. The question was reduced to technicalities rather than the propriety of a government's requiring private information from citizens for one purpose and then using it for another.

10

Subverting the Law

Many Canadians were shocked when they learned that members of the RCMP had engaged in illegal activities. The reality of outlaw policemen was so at variance with the childhood images of red-coated Mounties that some people refused to believe the early stories. The Mountie image, carefully cultivated for more than a hundred years, has served the force well whenever anyone dared to criticize it. Critics could easily be dismissed as disloyal Canadians. Journalists, who should be sceptics by inclination and training, felt for many years that the force was one institution that need not be questioned too closely. When the first stories of RCMP dirty tricks began to appear reporters and editors were the people who were put on the defensive and branded as scandalmongers who suffered from "Watergate envy." (In fact, the RCMP scandals were worse than Watergate in some ways. The Watergate break-in was conducted by a small group of political loyalists. In Canada we had numerous break-ins and other illegal acts conducted by all levels of the national police force.)

The image started to fade when the public learned from the testimony of Mounties that they had a cavalier approach to the law. Cpl. Dale Boire, who participated in the PQ tapes theft, testified that the force was "borrowing it more than stealing it. We were borrowing it for a couple of hours . . . if it was something

I was doing on my own on weekends I would think it was illegal." But because Operation Ham had headquarters approval, "it was kosher." Judge McDonald wondered if Boire felt free to disobey an illegal order. "If it was utterly ridiculous you wouldn't do it.... Logic would prevail then," Boire said. He also couldn't remember too much about the Criminal Code from his basic training days in Regina. But he could remember "a lot of riding ponies."

Insp. Joseph Nowlan, a headquarters officer who helped plan Operation Ham, said that this "surreptitious entry" was "similar to a breaking and entering" which was "not specifically provided for by law." But he said he wasn't required to assess the legality of it.

Cpl. Gerard Boucher, the lock-picking expert, said he was "just doing a job ... my training in the RCMP showed me to respect my superiors.... I had confidence in authority."

Howard Draper, the former deputy director-general who recommended Operation Ham, said he realized that the operation was putting the men in Montreal at some legal risk. The men were asked to do something "that was technically illegal," but that was "one of the crosses you bear when you're in a senior spot."

Paul Langlois, who was the RCMP driver in the interception of the toy store clerk, said he was always told "that the regulations of the RCMP commissioner have prevalence over any other act.... It was accepted in our circle."

To those who could remember the war crimes trials of Nazis these excuses had a chilling impact of *déjà vu*.

The Mountie image has also helped the force in its dealings with elected political leaders. Government officials who should have been watching what the force was up to abandoned their duty. When the scandals began to break and opposition parties started to demand explanations the governing Liberals were able to dodge the substantive issues by trying to paint the Tories and the NDP as being anti-Mountie. In his only major speech on the scandals in the 1979 election campaign, Conservative leader Joseph Clark travelled to Regina, the hometown of the RCMP, to accuse the Liberals of abandoning the Mounties in the grey area near the edge of the law. He dared not criticize the force itself. Tory MPs from western provinces, where the love of the force is the strongest, knew that attacking the Mounties was tantamount to committing political hari-kari. Parliamentarians have had opportunities to play watchdog to the national police. All too frequently they showed more interest in making sure that the Musical Ride would pay a visit to entertain their constituents. This atmosphere made it easy for Mounties to think they were beyond criticism and easier yet to cover up illegal activities.

In the early days of the scandals there was a general feeling that the Security Service was the dark side of the force. These were the clever boys who were let out of uniform to ply their spy craft, some felt. Despite its illegality and the horrible political implications, there was a grudging admiration for the precise planning and execution of Operation Ham, the break-in to get the PQ tapes. Donald Cobb's phoney communiqué was so good that it fooled other pros. Our boys were in there in the big league with the CIA and the Soviet KGB. The Security Service used classic techniques of disinformation and disruptive tactics. Internal security was protected with elaborate code and cypher systems. The "need-to-know" principle was a protection against leaks. To those familiar with the abundant literature on spy craft, none of this was new. The true test of a national security agency, however, is its ability to quickly identify the real threats and not to waste its time on legitimate dissenters. This the Security Service failed to do.

The outstanding example is the Security Service's inability to tell the difference between Quebec terrorists and those who advocate Quebec sovereignty through peaceful and democratic means. The labels were used in many internal documents to create one word—"separatist/terrorist." But there were other target groups as well. Warren Hart, an American black who worked as an FBI informer, has acknowledged that he was loaned to the RCMP to spy on black and native groups in Canada. Noel Starblanket, the president of the National Indian Brotherhood, says native people in Thunder Bay were approached by an RCMP agent provocateur with plans for stealing and hiding weapons. This same agent volunteered to teach British Columbia natives how to use military hardware and explosives. The Brotherhood obtained an affidavit from a Northern Ontario Indian who was recruited by the Security Service. He was paid $75 plus expenses to spy on "leftist" Indians at a Winnipeg meeting in September 1976. His pay was later raised to about $200 a month to provide regular information about employees of Grand Council Treaty No. 9 and other native groups. The Security Service was "especially interested in who was working for which organization, what organizations were doing and planning for the future, and the interrelationships between the various organizations," the man says. The Security Service wanted names so they could "check their political affiliations in the RCMP files." A Mountie "reported back to me that one of the employees was a leftist sympathizer and should be fired and asked me to talk to other employees about that person and put on pressure so that person would lose the employment. When I returned to Timmins, that person was no longer employed by Grand Council Treaty No. 9." This paid informer also reported that the president of the council was quitting to serve as an aide to Indian Affairs Minister Hugh Faulkner and gave an assessment of the likely candidate to assume the presidency.

Organized labour has also been an RCMP Security Service target. During the 1930s the secretary of the Regina Labour Council was an RCMP plant, according to Larry Brown, the executive director of the Saskatchewan Federation of Labour. Brown says that during the 1950s a stenographer at the Regina office of the Canadian Labour Congress admitted that she was an RCMP plant. "In 1965, in Saskatoon, one of the staff representatives who worked in the Saskatoon Union Centre, a person who was vulnerable to pressure because he was having emotional problems, was taken for a ride by two RCMP undercover agents. They asked him at that time to report to them on the political opinions of the people in the trade union movement," Brown says. "He was put under very heavy pressure. He refused to provide the information, but the pressures this emotionally vulnerable man was subjected to were sufficient that he wasn't able to show up at work for a week afterwards. And when he did show up for work again they asked him again and pressured him."

Brown says that staff representatives of a national union were getting so many requests to become RCMP informers that a bulletin was sent out asking people not to comply with Mountie approaches. Another union in Saskatchewan held a political philosophy course and "made the mistake" of teaching that there were systems in the world other than democratic capitalism. Participants in the course were shadowed in a "real Keystone Kops" method from restaurants to hotels, Brown says.

The Security Service didn't consider itself to be very funny even when Mounties bungled jobs such as the barn burning. The amateur torch team was in the same business as the PQ tapes theft crew. The only difference was the degree of sophistication. The single-minded determination to carry out a mission regardless of the legalities was also the hallmark of the force's Criminal Investigations Branch. Those who thought of the Security Service as a corrupt mutation of the RCMP had those illusions shattered when the McDonald Commission learned how the criminal investigators secretly obtained supposedly confidential information from tax and unemployment insurance files, conducted break-ins to plant bugs and carry out "intelligence probes" and opened mail in violation of the Post Office Act. These methods of operation were common throughout the force. There was an overwhelming lack of respect for the requirement to use legal methods. There was little or no accountability all the way up the line. Even when senior officers acknowledged to superiors that wiretaps were conducted in criminal cases in contravention of strict force policy there was no disciplinary action taken.

That lack of accountability extended to the political level. There is some evidence that the Mounties were at least uncomfortable with their illegal activities and tried to get the government to deal with the problem. The McDonald Commission learned that in 1970 the cabinet committee on priorities and planning received a report concerning possible lawbreaking by the Security Service in the line of duty. The report said, "It seems reasonably clear that this inherent contradiction has not been resolved and that an early solution must be found."

Two weeks after James Cross was released and his kidnappers were allowed to flee to Cuba a second committee, the cabinet committee on security and intelligence, received a report on

"RCMP strategy for dealing with the FLQ and other similar movements." This second report said that infiltrating FLQ cells would be a priority, but "the greatest bar to effective penetration by human sources is the problem raised by having members of the RCMP, or paid agents, commit serious crimes in order to establish bona fides with the members of the organization they are seeking to infiltrate. Among other things, this involves the difficult question of providing some kind of immunity from arrest and punishment of human sources. . . ." The report asked what the responsibility of the government should be to Mounties and agents who might be arrested "for committing a crime in the line of duty as it were." The report also said that "changes in existing legislation will be required if effective penetration by technical means (bugs) is to be achieved." The chairman of both those cabinet committees was Prime Minister Trudeau.

Trudeau and other ministers have maintained that they never knew the Mounties were acting illegally. Yet here were two reports that clearly imply that the Mounties considered it a problem even if the documents don't say explicitly what the force had been doing in the past. Nothing much seems to have happened with the two reports. The first report was discussed by the full cabinet, which then ordered a further study of this "contradiction" as well as "the atmosphere in which the law was administered." Further studies in Ottawa usually mean that the government hopes a problem will go away or at least disappear from sight. Trudeau deferred discussion of the second report and it never came up on the agenda of the security and intelligence committee again, according to John Starnes, who was present.

George McIlraith, who was solicitor-general at the time the reports were presented, said he was never told the RCMP was in fact breaking the law. He was aware of the dilemma, but he did nothing more, he told the McDonald Commission.

Higgitt and Starnes testified that solicitors-general must have known about illegal acts. "Nothing was hidden" from the ministers, Higgitt said. Starnes testified that a solicitor-general "would have to be an idiot" not to know. (That was a possibility, but not likely.) Starnes said that in a parliamentary democracy "I don't see how you can avoid having the buck stop with the minister."

But the buck was exactly what Trudeau and the ministers wanted to pass. Trudeau said ministers couldn't be held responsible for every little misdeed of every civil servant down the line. But this was the testimony of the most senior members of the RCMP—the commissioner and the director-general of the Security Service—who knew about illegalities and who were meeting regularly with the solicitor-general. This was institutionalized lawbreaking—a form of organized crime—and the ministers said they didn't know.

There is, however, another possible explanation for the professed ignorance of ministers and some senior RCMP officials regarding illegal activities. It can be the result of practising the policy of "need to know" regarding these activities. When only those who "need to know" are aware of illegal activities, higher-ups can later honestly deny knowledge of these activities. It was exactly this kind of arrangement Cobb unsuccessfully tried to forge with Starnes. Cobb, the field-unit commander, didn't want to tell the director-general what the men in G-section were up to so that if operations were exposed the senior officers of the force would remain untouched by the scandal. Jean-Pierre Goyer, McIlraith's successor, wanted to know who was being bugged and tapped, but word was sent back to the force via aide Robin Bourne that the solicitor-general didn't want to know how the bugs were installed. Would only "an idiot" not be able to figure out that you have to break into a place to plant a bug? Or could a solicitor-general figure out the truth and deliberately choose not to have it confirmed? Would you have to be "an idiot" not to suspect that a police force you knew was spying on the APLQ might have been responsible for the APLQ break-in and theft of documents? Or might you deliberately not ask so that you could honestly say later that you didn't know? The solicitors-general were lawyers who might be expected to know that the aiding and abetting section of the Criminal Code makes it an offence to do something to help, or to passively allow, someone else get away with a crime.

The various solicitors-general have given all kinds of excuses for not knowing what the RCMP was up to. John Turner said he probably didn't question the Mounties too closely about an apparent break-in operation because the briefing took place on his last day in the portfolio. George McIlraith said he suffered from failing eyesight and didn't read reports too carefully. Jean-Pierre Goyer said he didn't ask about the APLQ break-in because he just couldn't believe that the Mounties would break the law. Warren Allmand was told that there were "technical violations" of the law when Mounties obtained confidential tax information, but he didn't know what that meant and he didn't have enough time to find out. Francis Fox said the APLQ break-in was an isolated incident, but when he found out about others, such as Operation Ham, he tried to defend the force.

Fox's performance is particularly interesting because it goes to the very heart of the issue. In October 1977 it was Fox's unhappy task to tell the House of Commons about Operation Ham, the PQ tapes caper. He asked MPs to judge the episode in the "context of the times." That in itself was curious because Operation Ham took place two years after the October Crisis. But Fox drew most of his inspiration from a long-neglected Royal Commission report on security. The 1969 report has buried away in it one short passage which says, in part: "A security service will inevitably be involved in actions that may contravene the spirit if not the letter of the law...." That passage was largely ignored outside of the force until Fox trotted it out in 1977 to try to explain why Operation Ham took place. Fox said, "It will be noted that the Royal Commission did not say that a security service must never be involved in any actions 'that may contravene the spirit if not the letter of the law.' It would have been easy for the Royal Commission to say that." But in fact the Royal Commission *did* say that this particular Security Service should not be engaged in illegal activities because it was part of a police force. If Fox had not been afflicted with solicitors-general syndrome, a malady characterized by poor eyesight, he might have read the full sentence. The Royal Commission said: "A security service will inevitably be involved in actions that may contravene the spirit if not the letter of the law, and with clandestine and other activities which may sometimes seem to infringe on individuals' rights; these are not appropriate police functions."

The passage was part of a longer argument in favour of divorcing the Security Service from the RCMP, a recommendation that sent shock waves throughout the force and which was rejected by the Trudeau government. Yet bastardized versions of that passage were used not only by Fox, but also by Mounties trying to justify the unjustifiable. Moreover, the Royal Commission's view that protection of national security might involve bending if not breaking the law is an assumption that was never backed up with supporting evidence in the version of the report that was released publicly. (The full text of the report has never been released.) In rejecting the recommendation for a civilian agency the government appeared to be rejecting this argument. But the government found the argument handy after the RCMP was revealed as a lawless police force that was beyond control.

Even Trudeau, the former law school professor, tried to reduce Mountie lawbreaking to mere technical violations. He gave as examples a policeman exceeding the posted speed limit to catch a speeding motorist or a policeman who doesn't have time to get a warrant and decides he has to break into a house to prevent terrorists from detonating an A-bomb and destroying a city. The examples were irrational and absurd. There are existing provisions in highway traffic laws to permit policemen to exceed speed limits in pursuit of speeders or other wrongdoers. And the Criminal Code gives everyone, not just policemen, the power to use reasonable force to stop a crime that would likely "cause immediate and serious injury" to life or property. Furthermore, where was the ticking A-bomb in the APLQ offices? Where were the terrorists in the office of the company that handled the PQ data processing?

Yet some Mounties tried to use Trudeau's examples when they appeared before the McDonald Commission. Judge McDonald, usually patient to a fault, finally told one Mountie to stop using those bad examples.

But Fox and Trudeau were creating their justifications after the saga of lawbreaking had been revealed. What was going through the minds of Mounties at the time that they were engaged in illegal acts? Why would they so willingly put themselves in legal jeopardy by burning barns, conducting break-ins, tampering with mail, etc?

The McDonald Commission revealed an incredible series of

secret RCMP documents which may supply an important clue. They are so blatant that if they had been leaked to a newspaper in 1970, the time when they were written, they probably would have been dismissed as forgeries. But former Commissioner Higgitt confirmed their authenticity during his testimony.

The first is a classified memo dated June 23, 1970, from Assistant Adjutant D.K. Wilson to E.H. Stevenson, the RCMP's director of organization and personnel. Wilson explained that during a recent RCMP basic police personnel management-training course the subject of lawbreaking came up. "Talk also encompassed procedure followed where Criminal Code or other criminal or quasi-criminal legislation had been violated," Wilson wrote. "You will be aware that certain tasks performed by S.I.B. or C.I.B. personnel require that the law be transgressed, whether it be Federal, Provincial or Municipal law, in order that the purpose of the undertaking may be fulfilled. The particular task will have been sanctioned in many cases by a number of officers who will at least be aware of the means required to achieve the end product, and who will have given their tacit or express approval. Some of the means, if discovered, could result in criminal or civil process against the member(s) involved. It is not beyond the realm of possibility that the secret nature of the operation would preclude the Force from divulging any information to the authorities."

The class wanted to know, Wilson said, whether the force would stand by its men. "If it is necessary for a member to accept prosecution, what provisions are there for wife and family? Having been subjected to legal process, where does the member stand in terms of future employment?" One of the men in the class "went so far as to say that if there was no protection, and he knows it, he would be finished with his work forthwith." Wilson concluded by recommending that if there was a policy to protect Mounties there should be assurances "given to our members on a need-to-know basis." He was particularly concerned for men "engaged in highly sensitive or secret areas" on a regular basis. And "if this problem has not been considered that it now come under review and firm policy established."

Stevenson passed the memo along the line. It was seen by G.W. Mortimer, the deputy commissioner for administration, J.R.R.

Carrière, the deputy commissioner for criminal operations, and E.W. Willes, the director of criminal intelligence. Each man signed or initialed the document. It was sent to the RCMP legal branch for comment. On July 8 Staff Sgt. C.J.H. Kilburn of the legal branch returned the Wilson memo along with his own secret memo to Willes of criminal intelligence.

The legal branch did not suggest that Mounties should obey the law. Kilburn recommended instead that if a Mountie was caught in an operation that was sanctioned by a superior, "I feel that the member should be protected as much as possible internally from the rigour of a criminal or quasi-criminal responsibility. If a charge is laid, the Attorney-General should be approached with a view of staying the proceedings in the public interest. If the Attorney-General does not concur, then counsel should be supplied" by the RCMP "if the member acted reasonably." If the Mountie was convicted of an indictable offence the commissioner still "has a discretion whether to dismiss or not" and it "should be exercised in favour of retention of the member. Any fine should be paid by the Force and if sentenced to imprisonment, the Force should pay him as usual and he should be placed in a position of employment in the Force after his release. . . . If an unfortunate instance, such as outlined above, ever arose, and there is a great probability that it could, the position outlined above would be the only feasible way to cope with it — the interests of the member being served sufficiently to avert any civil liberty outcries and adverse reactions based on article(s) written as a result of the Force not 'standing by' him. There could be adverse reactions even if the Force 'stands by' the member, but I do not believe that it would attain the momentum of the instance where the member was not fully protected."

Kilburn said that if a member broke the law without the sanction of an officer the Mountie couldn't expect help "unless, under the particular circumstances of the case, the Force decided that he had, in spite of illegality, acted reasonably. . . . If so, he would be provided counsel. If he was convicted and sentenced . . . the Force would not have the same moral obligation to retain him."

Kilburn's note was forwarded to Deputy Commissioner Carrière who sent it along to Deputy Commissioner Mortimer with a secret memo of his own. Carrière wrote, "I am in agreement with the views expressed by the Legal Branch. . . . I feel however that this policy cannot be published in Policy Instructions, but suggest that it can best be handled by being made available to C.O.s Divisions and C.I.B. Officers, who would then be in a position to advise members when the subject is raised. In addition it is felt this information could be imparted to members attending" courses and seminars. "My view is that the information should be distributed on a 'need-to-know' basis in a confidential manner."

John Starnes, the director-general of the Security Service, was asked for his comments. His memo says he was "in agreement with the views expressed by the Legal Branch." He also wanted legal branch staff to brief Security Service members attending courses at headquarters about this protection policy because "in the past this problem of 'protection' has been raised on a number of occasions by members. . . ."

A draft letter to all commanding officers and Security Service officers was prepared for Higgitt's signature. It says: "Though it has not been the subject of general conversation, and should not be, it may have been considered necessary in the past, and may continue to be necessary in the future, to transgress the common, civil or criminal law of the Country in order to work effectively or to achieve the desired end results in a given case." Mounties engaged in "delicate operations" have expressed concerns for their protection if "an operation goes sour and they become subject to civil or criminal processes as a result." The letter described the protection policy of providing lawyers and promises to keep the pay cheques coming. The RCMP would pay fines and civil damage awards. The policy was secret and Mounties should be told of it only on a "need-to-know" basis. The letter said: "It must always be borne in mind, of course, that where a member is directed to perform a duty which may require him to contravene the law for any purpose or where the means required to achieve a specific end can reasonably be foreseen as illegal, a member is within his rights to refuse to do an unlawful act. Such a refusal may be given with impunity. Though no disciplinary action would be taken, a transfer may be indicated in such a situation."

Higgitt didn't want his signature on any document like that. He

There is the risk that indeed we may be too stupid to know what's good for us. But democracy means that we can change things when we are confronted with the facts and that we can weigh the risks and that we can decide for ourselves. We might, for example, feel that mandatory strip searches of all airline passengers too high a price to pay to prevent a hijacking. And we might later change our minds.

The RCMP's anti-democratic attitude robs us of the chance to decide things for ourselves and to make our own mistakes, if it comes to that. If the RCMP's view predominates, then we accept the risks that go with their arbitrary measures. We agree, for example, that the police are the only people qualified to decide when is more important to society to invade rather than respect privacy of the mail. And we agree to let the police make those decisions secret with no chance for the electorate to turf out people who might make the wrong decision. We abandon democracy.

One of the most pathetic aspects of the McDonald Commission proceedings has been that the RCMP has asked Canadians to permit police discretion, that is, arbitrary measures, on the flimsiest excuses. The arguments frequently have been cloaked in terms of "the need to protect national security."

What is national security? There can be general agreement that armed aggression by a foreign power is a threat to national security. But what of lesser threats? Is the democratic election of a separatist government in Quebec a threat to national security? There are strong arguments on both sides of that question. There plenty of room for honest disagreement. And the fact that there disagreement bolsters the argument for preserving the rule of law. Such honest disagreements can be arbitrated and adjudicated the courts. If Quebec Premier René Lévesque appears to engaged in illegal activity, sedition perhaps, he can face trial. That hasn't happened and Lévesque has always maintained he will try to achieve Quebec sovereignty through lawful and democratic means.

Threatening national security is not a crime. It's not mentioned the Criminal Code. Levying war is. Espionage is. Treason is. Sedition is. Acts of terrorism, such as kidnapping and plane hijacking, are also defined in the Criminal Code.

didn't sign it. Canadians might have expected that the commissioner of their national police force would have said something like, "Wait a minute. Our police will obey the law and if there's a problem with the law we'll try to get it changed." But Higgitt's handwritten note of July 31, 1970, says something quite different: "Under no circumstances should anything of this nature be circulated in written or memo form. The reasons ought to be obvious. I do not believe this is the problem it is being made out to be. Members know—or ought to—that whatever misadventure happens to them our Force will stand by them so long as there is *some* justification for doing so." Higgitt underlined the word "some."

Why Higgitt or somebody else didn't shred the documents will remain one of those mysteries. Deputy Commissioner Mortimer instructed Stevenson of organization and personnel to put the documents "in [the] secret envelope on policy file." The "contents to be relayed to S and I and C.I.B. classes orally when [they] convene at HQ Ottawa." The men in Security and Intelligence and Criminal Investigations Branch classes were to be told that they could expect legal and financial protection for their lawbreaking and that if they refused to obey an illegal order they could be transferred.

What the documents reveal is a police force that clearly believed it was beyond the law. The most senior officers felt "misadventures" could be cleared up with a friendly little chat with the provincial attorney-general. And if that didn't work the boys could be protected by legal counsel provided by the force. If worse came to worse the wives and kids would be looked after and when jailbird Mounties served their time they would be welcomed back with open arms.

Are the Mounties beyond the law? Donald Cobb is the only Mountie who has stood trial on charges related to recent Mountie illegal activities and after his plea of guilty he went back to headquarters without any demotion. We will not know what will happen with the other Mounties until the McDonald Commission makes its final report. If the commission fails to recommend legal and disciplinary action the message will be clear that it's okay for Mounties to break the law. The McDonald Commission could be seen as the same kind of vindication that the Mounties felt they received from the earlier Royal Commission. But the McDonald Commission could also become the first clear and authoritative voice in years to inform the RCMP that the rule of law still applies in Canada.

The issue of RCMP illegal activities never got a thorough airing during the 1979 federal election campaign. Trudeau tried to dodge the issue of possible cabinet culpability by pleading memory loss. He told a press conference that he couldn't really remember any details of the reports received by the committees he chaired—the reports that raised the intriguing questions of what might happen if Mounties or their agents felt they had to break the law in the "line of duty."

Tory leader Joe Clark raised the issue only briefly when he spoke in Regina and promised that his government would provide a "framework" whereby the RCMP might break the law in extraordinary cases if prior approval is obtained from a cabinet minister. Clark's plan calls for an after-the-fact review of such situations by an all-party committee of parliamentarians. New Democratic Party leader Ed Broadbent alone called for the police to obey the law.

The limited national "debate" failed to focus on the most essential of questions. Is there ever a time when the rule of law should be curtailed in the greater national interest? To adequately discuss such a question one must review some basic principles of democracy. The rule of law, the principle that everyone is subject to the same processes of law, is fundamental to a parliamentary democracy. There is no preamble to the Criminal Code which says that it doesn't apply to policemen or any other class of citizens or that it doesn't apply when a cabinet minister says so. The powers of peace officers are very carefully delineated. Canadian lawmakers, and legislators in most other democracies, have tried to circumscribe police powers and to eliminate discretion which may easily turn to abuse.

In the case of wiretapping, for example, Parliament felt that this was a tool needed by police to identify criminals and gather evidence of crimes. Even if the wiretap debate resulted in some erroneous conclusions about the value of this tool, the point is that a legal structure was established for controlling and regulating

electronic invasion of privacy. Elected representativ portunity to weigh and measure two values—the privacy and the need to apprehend criminals. T tried to strike a balance between those sometimes ues. If society felt that its elected representatives that balance there was an opportunity to expres the polls.

The RCMP has shown that it doesn't always mocracy operates. When its view of what th hasn't prevailed the force has ignored the e RCMP, however, doesn't exist to try to strike conflicting values. That's the job of Parliament ently recognizes this. Witness the elaborate se illegal activities. The potential for scandal wa less, the force decided to take the law into its belief that it alone knew what was best for th the RCMP was saying to Parliament and the are too stupid to know what's good for you."

Members of the force argue that circums which extraordinary measures must be taken greater good. Some Mounties have said that sibly anticipate and legislate for every cont ments have been diminished by the fact th able to point to a single example that has examination. But assume for the moment some unanticipated flaw in the law and s criminal or murderous terrorist might be the RCMP was constrained. What is the pay? Might we see two hundred passen jacked jetliner lose their lives? Such an ev the sensibilities of all Canadians, and it pressures needed to produce new laws to

A strict adherence to the rule of law p rule of law protects each of us individua arbitrary measures that may be impos agents. That, too, is worth something. between abandoning the principle of th a hypothetical tragedy. There are certa didn't sign it. Canadians might have expected that the commissioner of their national police force would have said something like, "Wait a minute. Our police will obey the law and if there's a problem with the law we'll try to get it changed." But Higgitt's handwritten note of July 31, 1970, says something quite different: "Under no circumstances should anything of this nature be circulated in written or memo form. The reasons ought to be obvious. I do not believe this is the problem it is being made out to be. Members know—or ought to—that whatever misadventure happens to them our Force will stand by them so long as there is *some* justification for doing so." Higgitt underlined the word "some."

Why Higgitt or somebody else didn't shred the documents will remain one of those mysteries. Deputy Commissioner Mortimer instructed Stevenson of organization and personnel to put the documents "in [the] secret envelope on policy file." The "contents to be relayed to S and I and C.I.B. classes orally when [they] convene at HQ Ottawa." The men in Security and Intelligence and Criminal Investigations Branch classes were to be told that they could expect legal and financial protection for their lawbreaking and that if they refused to obey an illegal order they could be transferred.

What the documents reveal is a police force that clearly believed it was beyond the law. The most senior officers felt "misadventures" could be cleared up with a friendly little chat with the provincial attorney-general. And if that didn't work the boys could be protected by legal counsel provided by the force. If worse came to worse the wives and kids would be looked after and when jailbird Mounties served their time they would be welcomed back with open arms.

Are the Mounties beyond the law? Donald Cobb is the only Mountie who has stood trial on charges related to recent Mountie illegal activities and after his plea of guilty he went back to headquarters without any demotion. We will not know what will happen with the other Mounties until the McDonald Commission makes its final report. If the commission fails to recommend legal and disciplinary action the message will be clear that it's okay for Mounties to break the law. The McDonald Commission could be seen as the same kind of vindication that the Mounties felt they received from the earlier Royal Commission. But the McDonald Commission could also become the first clear and authoritative voice in years to inform the RCMP that the rule of law still applies in Canada.

The issue of RCMP illegal activities never got a thorough airing during the 1979 federal election campaign. Trudeau tried to dodge the issue of possible cabinet culpability by pleading memory loss. He told a press conference that he couldn't really remember any details of the reports received by the committees he chaired—the reports that raised the intriguing questions of what might happen if Mounties or their agents felt they had to break the law in the "line of duty."

Tory leader Joe Clark raised the issue only briefly when he spoke in Regina and promised that his government would provide a "framework" whereby the RCMP might break the law in extraordinary cases if prior approval is obtained from a cabinet minister. Clark's plan calls for an after-the-fact review of such situations by an all-party committee of parliamentarians. New Democratic Party leader Ed Broadbent alone called for the police to obey the law.

The limited national "debate" failed to focus on the most essential of questions. Is there ever a time when the rule of law should be curtailed in the greater national interest? To adequately discuss such a question one must review some basic principles of democracy. The rule of law, the principle that everyone is subject to the same processes of law, is fundamental to a parliamentary democracy. There is no preamble to the Criminal Code which says that it doesn't apply to policemen or any other class of citizens or that it doesn't apply when a cabinet minister says so. The powers of peace officers are very carefully delineated. Canadian lawmakers, and legislators in most other democracies, have tried to circumscribe police powers and to eliminate discretion which may easily turn to abuse.

In the case of wiretapping, for example, Parliament felt that this was a tool needed by police to identify criminals and gather evidence of crimes. Even if the wiretap debate resulted in some erroneous conclusions about the value of this tool, the point is that a legal structure was established for controlling and regulating electronic invasion of privacy. Elected representatives had the opportunity to weigh and measure two values—the need to protect privacy and the need to apprehend criminals. The wiretap law tried to strike a balance between those sometimes conflicting values. If society felt that its elected representatives erred in striking that balance there was an opportunity to express displeasure at the polls.

The RCMP has shown that it doesn't always like the way democracy operates. When its view of what the law should be hasn't prevailed the force has ignored the existing law. The RCMP, however, doesn't exist to try to strike balances between conflicting values. That's the job of Parliament. The force apparently recognizes this. Witness the elaborate secrecy surrounding illegal activities. The potential for scandal was great. Nevertheless, the force decided to take the law into its own hands in the belief that it alone knew what was best for the country. In effect, the RCMP was saying to Parliament and the public: "You people are too stupid to know what's good for you."

Members of the force argue that circumstances may arise in which extraordinary measures must be taken in order to serve the greater good. Some Mounties have said that lawmakers can't possibly anticipate and legislate for every contingency. Their arguments have been diminished by the fact that they haven't been able to point to a single example that has held up under close examination. But assume for the moment that there might be some unanticipated flaw in the law and somehow a dangerous criminal or murderous terrorist might be able to slip by because the RCMP was constrained. What is the price we might have to pay? Might we see two hundred passengers trapped on a hijacked jetliner lose their lives? Such an event would surely shock the sensibilities of all Canadians, and it would also generate the pressures needed to produce new laws to cover that situation.

A strict adherence to the rule of law preserves a principle. The rule of law protects each of us individually and collectively from arbitrary measures that may be imposed by the state and its agents. That, too, is worth something. The choice, therefore, is between abandoning the principle of the rule of law and averting a hypothetical tragedy. There are certain risks in a democracy.

There is the risk that indeed we may be too stupid to know what's good for us. But democracy means that we can change things when we are confronted with the facts and that we can weigh the risks and that we can decide for ourselves. We might, for example, feel that mandatory strip searches of all airline passengers is too high a price to pay to prevent a hijacking. And we might later change our minds.

The RCMP's anti-democratic attitude robs us of the chance to decide things for ourselves and to make our own mistakes, if it comes to that. If the RCMP's view predominates, then we accept the risks that go with their arbitrary measures. We agree, for example, that the police are the only people qualified to decide when it is more important to society to invade rather than respect privacy of the mail. And we agree to let the police make those decisions in secret with no chance for the electorate to turf out people who might make the wrong decision. We abandon democracy.

One of the most pathetic aspects of the McDonald Commission proceedings has been that the RCMP has asked Canadians to permit police discretion, that is, arbitrary measures, on the flimsiest of excuses. The arguments frequently have been cloaked in terms like "the need to protect national security."

What is national security? There can be general agreement that armed aggression by a foreign power is a threat to national security. But what of lesser threats? Is the democratic election of a separatist government in Quebec a threat to national security? There are strong arguments on both sides of that question. There is plenty of room for honest disagreement. And the fact that there is disagreement bolsters the argument for preserving the rule of law. Such honest disagreements can be arbitrated and adjudicated by the courts. If Quebec Premier René Lévesque appears to have engaged in illegal activity, sedition perhaps, he can face trial. But that hasn't happened and Lévesque has always maintained that he will try to achieve Quebec sovereignty through lawful and democratic means.

Threatening national security is not a crime. It's not mentioned in the Criminal Code. Levying war is. Espionage is. Treason is. Sedition is. Acts of terrorism, such as kidnapping and plane hijacking, are also defined in the Criminal Code.

The question then arises, should the RCMP be involved in protecting an ambiguous notion of national security? Or should the force stick to enforcing the defined law and in that way serve national security? The Security Service ignores the law enforcement function of police and devotes almost its entire energy to national security, whatever the current definition of that term may be.

The dangers here are obvious. The police are left to define the good guys and the bad guys, to decide on who are potential subversives, who are appropriate targets for Security Service attention. Once defined as a threat to national security, an individual can be subjected to the most damaging invasions of his privacy. And for what purpose? To bring him to justice for illegal activities? Not necessairly, as McDonald Commission testimony has established. It's often only to justify further investigation. Donald Cobb said, "A Security Service is like a research organization.... We may open an investigation on a thousand people with former Communist party links because among those may be a long-term penetration agent."

There seem to be much more compelling arguments for the RCMP to confine itself to investigating defined crimes. Specific illegal acts or suspected acts can be investigated with the view of eventually launching a prosecution. There is the final safeguard of the courts to protect individuals against police abuses or bad judgment calls.

But as the situation now stands individuals targetted for security investigation may or may not be criminals. Bad guys are bad guys because the police say so. They become quasi-criminals with no opportunity to clear their names. There might be some justification for this as part of the RCMP intelligence-gathering function. A bad guy might wait for months or years before he does anything criminal for which he can be prosecuted. There have been documented cases in the U.S. and Europe where an espionage agent has used a deep cover and waited for several years before he began spying. But the RCMP has a pretty poor track record in identifying these kinds of targets. There have been the obvious ones, such as the Soviet diplomatic staff in Ottawa. But on the domestic subversion front the Security Service consistently has failed to distinguish between legitimate dissent and criminal activity.

Labour unions, for example, have from time to time come under close scrutiny by the Security Service. So have groups of native people. So have student groups. The only common denominator seems to be that these groups have tried to disturb the status quo. And what's wrong with that? Everyone who votes against the governing party at election time is trying to disturb the status quo. If these groups remain within the law they deserve the protection of the police. Instead, they have become bad guys.

The targetting of groups, as opposed to individuals, often can lead to guilt by association. It invites faulty logic of this sort. Mr. Smith is a suspected subversive. He belongs to the All-Star Bowling League. Mr. Jones, another suspected subversive, also belongs to the league. Mr. Brown belongs to the league too. It seems to be a subversive organization. Therefore Mr. Brown is probably a subversive.

The example may seem far-fetched, but the evidence surrounding Operation Ham suggests that exactly this was happening to the Parti Québécois. The PQ was considered a subversive organization by the Security Service. It was subjected to Operation Ham. The object of that break-in wasn't to obtain evidence of any illegal activity. The object was to get PQ membership lists. Why? It seems safe to assume that Ham was an attempt to identify all the "subversives" who belonged to the PQ. Yet the Parti Québécois was not an illegal organization, nor had the Security Service established any grounds for laying any charges against any of its members.

Most groups of any size probably have members who have engaged in illegal activities or have contemplated doing so. By pointing to those individuals the RCMP can label a group as subversive and subject all of its members to investigation. And how many members of the Canadian Legion or the Newspaper Guild or the Kinsmen might like the possibility that because one of the members of the organization is disreputable or possibly crooked they all become suspect? If a group isn't labelled as a "front" it might be labelled by the RCMP as an innocent group subject to subversive "infiltration." In either case all of the members become suspect. By the operational principles of the Security Service, however, the group and its members become targets for the kinds of operations—including disruptive tactics, recruitment of informers, wiretaps, bugs and mail openings—which are apparently the standard procedures in the investigations of the Security Service.

The time has come for the RCMP and Canada's Security Service, wherever it may be located in the government structure, to concentrate on investigating real crimes, defined by our lawmakers. The McDonald Commission was told that a suspected subversive or spy isn't necessarily eliminated as a suspect even when a Security Service break-in fails to turn up any evidence. The suspect may be too cunning and clever. It seems to have escaped the force that there is a second possibility. Maybe the suspect is innocent. Yet as the Security Service now operates innocent people may be investigated for months or years before they're ever cleared, if indeed they are ever cleared.

In normal police practice an investigation is abandoned after a certain period of time when there isn't enough evidence to justify further work. The Security Service doesn't face this constraint. The Security Service isn't expected to justify its use of manpower and resources. Taxpayers might well ask if their money is being used wisely. If the Security Service is uncovering all kinds of illegal activities that are threatening to national security, where are the results? When was the last time a member of the Security Service was involved in a successful investigation leading to prosecution and conviction? Even with the sweeping scope of the Official Secrets Act, there has been only one successful prosecution in Canada under that act in the last twenty years. The handful of other Official Secrets Act prosecutions were thrown out of court for lack of evidence or the conviction was reversed on appeal. Are Canadian taxpayers financing a little boys' game of "I spy?" Or are they financing a political police whose real function, whether acknowledged or not by the federal government, has been to protect the political status quo from any serious threat? In the eyes of the Security Service, there appears to be no significant distinction between the small groups like the FLQ which did use illegal means and violence to promote their aims, and democratic and law-abiding political parties, labour unions and other organizations who seek changes in the political and economic status quo by legal means. The McDonald Commission has finally forced Canadians to address directly the question of whether a Security Service should be able to take away the political rights all citizens enjoy under the rule of law. It also forces us to deal seriously with the question of the role, the responsibilities and the limits to be placed on a security service in a parliamentary democracy.

No doubt Canada has its fair share of real terrorists, subversives and spys. Yet we have heard no convincing evidence from the RCMP that our existing laws are inadequate to deal with them. And even when the RCMP has broken the law in its hunt for national security threats, it has not been able to produce much to show for or justify such efforts.

Appendices

Appendix A

The Chain of Command—Operation Bricole

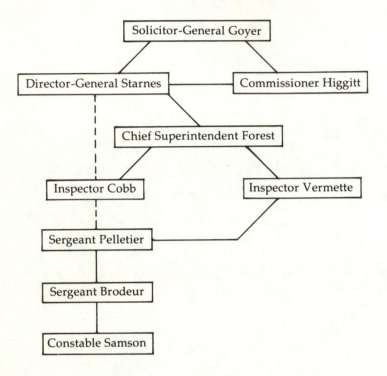

——— solid lines—normal reporting channels
— — — dotted lines—actual reporting channels for this operation

Appendix B

Operation Ham—Chain of Command

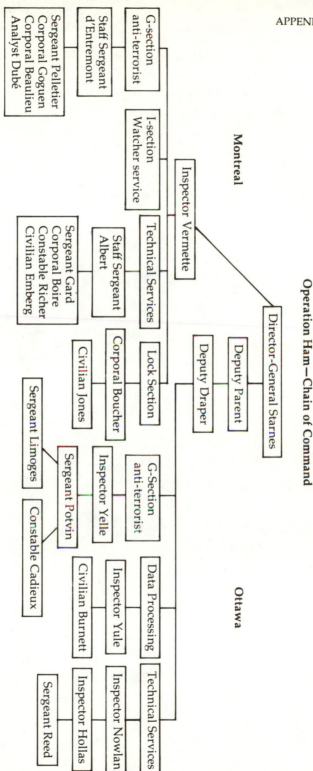

Index

201